THE BEST
100
PASTA DISHES
AND SAUCES

THE BEST
100
PASTA DISHES
AND SAUCES

A fabulous collection of classic
and contemporary pasta recipes

EBURY PRESS
LONDON

First published in the United Kingdom in 2000

1 3 5 7 9 10 8 6 4 2

Text and photography © The Random House Group Limited, 2000

First published by Ebury Press
Random House, 20 Vauxhall Bridge Road, London SW1V 2SA

Random House Australia (Pty) Limited
20 Alfred Street, Milsons Point, Sydney, New South Wales 2061,
Australia

Random House New Zealand Limited
18 Poland Road, Glenfield, Auckland 10, New Zealand

Random House South Africa (Pty) Limited
Endulini, 5A Jubilee Road, Parktown 2193, South Africa

The Random House Group Limited Reg. No. 954009

www.randomhouse.co.uk

A CIP catalogue record for this book is available from the
British Library.

Editor: Nicky Thompson
Designers: Christine and Paul Wood

ISBN 0 09 187832 2

Papers used by Ebury Press are natural, recyclable products made
from wood grown in sustainable forests.

Colour separation in Milan by Colorlito
Printed and bound in Spain by Graficas Estella

COOKERY NOTES

● Both metric and imperial measures are given for the recipes. Follow either set of measures, but not a mixture of both as they are not interchangeable.

● All spoon measures are level unless otherwise stated. Sets of measuring spoons are available in metric and imperial for accurate measurement of small quantities.

● Ovens should be preheated to the specified temperature. Grills should also be preheated. The cooking times given in the recipes assume that this has been done.

● Use large eggs except where otherwise specified. Free-range eggs are recommended.

● Use freshly ground black pepper and sea salt unless otherwise specified.

● If stocks are required, they should be freshly made when possible. Alternatively, buy ready-made stocks or use good-quality stock cubes.

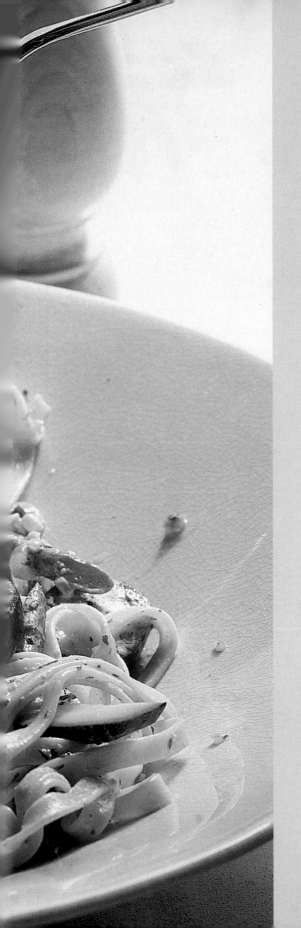

CONTENTS

INTRODUCTION

In Italy, hardly a meal is served without pasta and elsewhere in the world pasta has become incredibly popular. It is, after all, inexpensive, quick to cook and extremely versatile. The range of dried and fresh pastas readily available from supermarkets and delicatessens today is seemingly endless and, of course, you can combine these with all manner of tasty sauces.

From a nutritional angle, pasta is essentially a carbohydrate food but, because it has a low fat content, pasta isn't particularly high in calories. It's the accompanying sauces that make the recipes fattening; so if you are watching your weight, use low-calorie ingredients, such as vegetables, skimmed milk and low-fat cheese to replace full-fat ingredients, and keep the use of ingredients like olive oil, butter and olives to a minimum. Some varieties of pasta, notably those made with eggs, contain as much as 13% protein, as well as useful vitamins and minerals.

HOMEMADE PASTA

Although the availability of commercial fresh pastas is ever-increasing, there is no real substitute for homemade pasta. It is surprisingly quick and rewarding to make, and has a wonderfully light texture and an incomparable flavour – almost melting in the mouth. If you have never tried to make your own pasta, do have a go, using the recipe for pasta dough on page 12.

You need very little basic equipment – a rolling pin, metal pastry cutters, a sharp knife and a pastry wheel will suffice – but, if you intend to make pasta regularly, it's worth investing in a pasta machine to take all the hard work out of rolling and cutting. A pasta machine will also ensure that the dough is even and very thin, giving excellent results.

Once you have mastered the basic recipe, try your hand at some of the flavoured pastas (see pages 13–14). They are just as easy to make as basic pasta and give quite delicious results.

BOUGHT FRESH PASTA

Many supermarkets and Italian delicatessens now sell fresh pasta. If you prefer to buy fresh pasta rather than make your own or use dried, it is worth searching out a good supplier. Commercially produced fresh pasta tends to be unpleasantly thick and stodgy – quite unlike homemade pasta. However, Italian delicatessens often sell good-quality pasta (which has been freshly prepared on the premises) in an interesting range of flavours.

DRIED PASTA

Dried pasta is available in an extensive range of shapes, sizes and flavours. The best are made from 100% durum wheat (*pasta di semola grano duro*); some include eggs (*all'uova*). With the exception of filled pastas, such as ravioli, dried pasta is suitable for all the recipes in this book.

The variety of dried pasta shapes is almost bewildering. The names of shapes often vary from one region of Italy to another, and new ones are constantly being introduced. Below is a guide to the most common types, but this list is not exhaustive. It is useful to remember that the suffix gives an indication of the size of the pasta. *Oni* denotes large, as in conchiglioni (large shells); -*ette* or -*etti* suggests small, as in spaghetti and capelletti (small hats); while -*ine* or -*ini* means tiny as in pastina (tiny soup pasta) and spaghettini, the finer version of spaghetti.

COMMON PASTA SHAPES

Spaghetti: long, thin straight strands, available in slightly differing thicknesses. Spaghettini is a finer version of spaghetti; linguine is very slightly thicker. Bucatini is a thicker version.

Macaroni: thicker, tubular pasta, available in long and short lengths, often slightly curved, sometimes ridged. Short kinds include penne, tubetti and zite.

Vermicelli: very fine pasta strands, thinner than spaghetti, usually sold in nests; capelli d'angelo (angel's hair) is similar. Paglia e fino (straw and hay) are nests of fine plain egg and green pasta.

Noodles: narrow, flat egg pasta strips of varying widths, straight and coiled into nests; some with attractive wavy edges. Pappardelle are the broadest noodles. Tagliatelle and fettucine are the most common types. Not all noodles are made from pasta flour; oriental noodles, for example, are often made from rice flour or mung beans.

Lasagne: flat sheets of pasta, available in broad strips, rectangles and squares, straight or wavy edged. Usually made with egg pasta; lasagne verde (spinach pasta) is widely available too. Used in oven-baked dishes; some varieties do not require pre-cooking before baking. Lasagnette is a narrower version which is currently a popular alternative to tagliatelle.

Cannelloni are large hollow tubes of egg pasta which are typically filled with a stuffing and baked. Rigatoni are narrower tubes.

Stuffed pasta shapes: these include ravioli (squares) and raviolini (semi-circles), which may have plain or serrated edges. Tortelloni are made from stuffed rounds or squares, which are especially folded to give their characteristic shape.

Small pasta shapes: these are numerous and include capalletti (little hats); cavatappi (short ridged twists); conchiglie (shells); farfalle (bows); fusilli (twists); lumache (snails); orecchiette (ears); pipe (curved tubes); rotelle (wheels); and torchiette (torches).

Pastina: tiny pasta shapes used mainly in soups. These include corallini (rings); orzo or puntalette (rice grain shapes); and stellette (stars).

CHOICE OF SHAPES AND SIZES

The choice of pasta is largely a matter of personal taste, but you will find that some pasta shapes are more suited to particular recipes than others. Large shapes and wide noodles, for example, tend to work best in dishes where the other ingredients are chunky. Smoother-textured sauces are generally better served with finer pastas, such as spaghetti or linguine. Where a recipe includes a lot of sauce, shapes such as shells and tubes are ideal because they hold the sauce well.

QUANTITIES

It is difficult to give specific quantity guidelines for pasta, because there are so many factors, including the nature of the sauce and whether you are serving

the pasta as a starter, light lunch or main meal. Individual appetites for pasta seem to vary enormously too. As a very approximate guide, allow about 75–125g (3–4oz) uncooked weight per person.

COOKING PASTA

All pasta, fresh and dried, should be cooked until it is *al dente* – firm to the bite, definitely not soft, and without a hard, uncooked centre. Always add pasta to a large pan containing plenty of fast-boiling water; insufficient water will result in stodgy unevenly cooked pasta. Fresh pasta needs only the briefest of cooking, so watch it carefully. Most dried pasta takes around 8–12 minutes. Manufacturers' recommended cooking times provide a rough guide, but the only way to determine when pasta is cooked is by tasting. So use a fork to try a piece of pasta; if it is not ready, leave it to cook for a little longer and then test again. Avoid overcooking at all costs!

SERVING SUGGESTIONS

Have warmed serving plates or bowls ready as pasta quickly loses its heat once it is drained. Toss the pasta with the chosen sauce, butter or olive oil as soon as it is cooked, or it may start to stick together. If on the other hand you are cooking pasta to serve cold, drain and rinse with cold water to prevent further cooking and rinse off surface starch.

Parmesan cheese is almost an essential finishing touch to most pasta dishes. It may be expensive but a little goes a long way, and a well-wrapped chunk of Parmesan will keep in the refrigerator for several weeks. (Vegetarian Parmesan is available from healthfood shops.) Either grate the Parmesan over the finished dish or shave off thin flakes, using a swivel potato peeler or a special cheese grater.

Some of the most popular and readily available types of dried pasta are shown overleaf. They are:
1 cannelloni, 2 rigatoni, 3 long fusilli, 4 pastina,
5 conchiglioni, 6 tagliatelle, 7 pappardelle,
8 capalletti, 9 corallini, 10 lasagnette, 11 torchiette,
12 bucatini, 13 spaghetti, 14 spaghettini and 15 fusilli.

BEST FRESH PASTA RECIPES

Pasta dough can either be made by hand, in a food processor with a dough attachment, or in a large mixer with a dough hook. Initially, it is probably best to make the dough by hand to learn how the dough should feel at each stage. The more you make fresh pasta, the easier it will be to judge the correct texture of the dough – it should be soft, not at all sticky, and with a good elasticity.

The best type of flour to use for making pasta is a very fine wheat flour 'type 00' or 'farino tipo 00', which is available from Italian delicatessens and most larger supermarkets. Strong plain flour can be used as a substitute if necessary, although you may need to add a little more or less water.

Take care to avoid overcooking pasta. The only way to ensure that fresh or dried pasta is properly cooked is to taste it. Before the end of the recommended cooking time, take a piece of pasta from the cooking pan and bite it – it should be *al dente*, just tender but still firm to the bite. Fresh pasta takes 2–3 minutes, while dried pasta takes 8–12 minutes (use the packet instructions as a guide).

BASIC PASTA DOUGH

Serves 4
Preparation: 5 minutes, plus kneading
Cooking time: 1–2 minutes
Freezing: not suitable
285 cals per serving

225g (8oz) 'type 00' pasta flour, plus extra for dusting

5ml (1 tsp) salt

2 eggs, plus 1 egg yolk, beaten

15ml (1 tbsp) extra-virgin olive oil

15–30ml (1–2 tbsp) cold water

1 Sift the flour and salt into a mound on a clean surface. Make a well in the centre and add the eggs, egg yolk, oil and 15ml (1 tbsp) water.

2 Using a fork, gently beat the eggs together, then

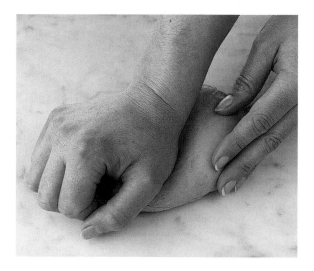

gradually work in the flour, adding a little extra water if necessary, to form a soft but not sticky dough.

3 Transfer the dough to a lightly floured surface and knead for about 5 minutes until the dough is firm, smooth and elastic.

4 Form the dough into a flattish ball, wrap in cling film and leave to rest in the refrigerator for at least 30 minutes.

USING A FOOD PROCESSOR

Sift the flour and salt into the processor bowl and add the eggs, egg yolk, oil and 15ml (1 tbsp) water (together with any flavourings). Process just until the dough begins to come together, adding extra water if

necessary, to form a soft but not sticky dough. Wrap in cling film and leave it to rest (as described above).

VARIATIONS

Flavoured pastas are easy to make and are delicious. Vegetable purées and flavoured pastes make vibrant coloured pastas – note that some of the colour will be lost during cooking, without detriment to the flavour.

BEETROOT PASTA

Purée 25g (1oz) cooked beetroot until very smooth and pass through a sieve, if necessary. Sift the flour and salt into a bowl, then gradually work in the beetroot paste with the rest of the ingredients, omitting the water. Continue as above.

BLACK PEPPERCORN PASTA

Sift the flour and salt into a bowl. Roughly crush 10ml (2 tsp) black peppercorns using a pestle and mortar or spice grinder. Stir into the flour and continue as above.

BUCKWHEAT PASTA

Sift 150g (5oz) 'type 00' pasta flour and the salt into a bowl, then stir in 75g (3oz) buckwheat flour. Increase the amount of water to 30–45ml (2–3 tbsp) and continue to work in the rest of the ingredients as above.

FRESH HERB PASTA

Sift the flour and salt into the bowl and stir in 45ml (3 tbsp) freshly chopped mixed herbs, such as basil, marjoram and parsley. Continue as above.

GARLIC AND BASIL PASTA

Sift the flour and salt into a bowl, stir in 15g (½oz) freshly chopped basil and 1 small crushed garlic clove. Continue as above.

LEMON PASTA

Sift the flour and salt into a bowl, then stir in the finely grated rind of 2 unwaxed lemons. Continue as above, replacing the water with 30ml (2 tbsp) lemon juice.

OLIVE PASTA

Beat the eggs with 30ml (2 tbsp) black olive paste before adding to the flour. You need less liquid so reduce the water to about 10ml (2 tsp). Continue as for basic pasta.

SAFFRON PASTA

Sift the flour and salt into a bowl and stir in 5ml (1 tsp) saffron strands. Continue as for basic pasta.

SPINACH PASTA

Blanch 50g (2oz) spinach leaves in a little boiling water until just wilted. Refresh under cold water, drain thoroughly and squeeze out all excess water, then finely chop the spinach. Add to the flour and salt, together with the remaining ingredients. Continue as for basic pasta.

SQUID INK PASTA

Add one sachet of squid ink to the beaten eggs before adding to the flour. Reduce the water to about 10ml (2 tsp). Continue as for basic pasta.

SUN-DRIED TOMATO PASTA

Beat the eggs with 30ml (2 tbsp) sun-dried tomato paste before adding to the flour. Reduce the water to about 10ml (2 tsp) and continue as above.

To make your own sun-dried tomato paste, purée the contents of a jar of sun-dried tomatoes in oil. Drain off a little oil first to get a good thick paste. Return the paste to the empty jar and store in the refrigerator.

ROLLING OUT DOUGH
USING A PASTA MACHINE

Most pasta machines work in the same way and the following method should apply. However, do refer to the manufacturer's instructions for your model.

1 Slice off about one-fifth of the dough. Re-wrap the rest in cling film so it does not dry out. Flatten the dough slightly by hand to fit in the machine. Starting with the machine set to roll at the thickest setting (ie rollers widest apart) pass the dough through the machine.

2 Fold the strip of dough in three, rotate and pass through the machine again. Repeat the folding and, with the rollers at this widest setting, pass the dough through once more. The dough should now be smooth and of an even thickness.

3 Adjust the setting of the rollers by one notch. Guide the dough through the machine using your hands. Do not pull the dough or it may drag and tear; let the machine dictate the pace.

4 Pass the dough through the machine once at each narrower setting, working through to the thinnest possible. Don't be tempted to skip a setting in order to save time, or the dough may drag and tear. The dough should gradually be rolled out to a very thin large sheet. See drying and cutting (pages 16–19). Repeat with the remaining dough.

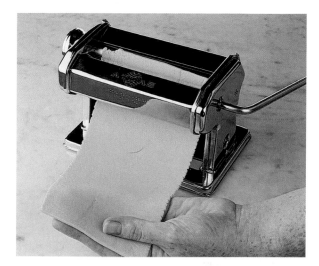

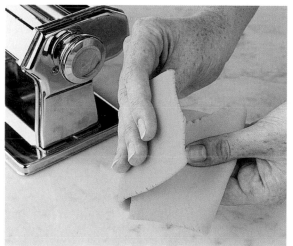

ROLLING OUT PASTA BY HAND

1 On a clean (not floured) surface, roll out one-third of the dough to a 5mm (¼ inch) thickness.

2 Lift the dough from the surface and rotate it by 45°. The dough should cling (not stick) to the surface; this helps in the stretching process.

3 Continue rolling, lifting and rotating until the dough is very thin. Repeat with remaining dough.

ALLOWING PASTA TO DRY

If you are making lasagne or stuffed pastas, such as ravioli or raviolini, the rolled pasta should be used immediately. Otherwise, drape the dough on a clean tea towel and leave to dry for 5–10 minutes before cutting. This makes it easier to cut and prevents the strands of pasta sticking together. Do not over-dry.

CUTTING PASTA RIBBONS BY MACHINE

Most pasta machines have tagliatelle and spaghetti cutter attachments. Do check with the instructions for your particular machine.

1 To cut tagliatelle, fit the appropriate attachment to the machine. Cut the pasta sheets into 25–30cm (10–12 inch) lengths. Pass these through the machine.

2 To cut spaghetti, fit the appropriate attachment to the machine. Cut the pasta sheets into lengths and pass through the machine as for tagliatelle.

CUTTING PASTA RIBBONS BY HAND

1 Loosely roll up sheets of pasta, like a mini Swiss roll.

2 Using a sharp knife, cut the rolled pasta into slices, the thickness depending on the type of pasta ribbons required. Use the following as a guide:

linguine – 5mm (¼ inch)

tagliatelle – 8mm (⅓ inch)

pappardelle – 2cm (¾ inch)

3 Carefully unravel the pasta ribbons by hand, taking care not to tear them.

4 Alternatively, cut pappardelle from a pasta sheet. Using a pastry wheel, plain or fluted, cut into strips about 2cm (¾ inch) wide.

LASAGNE AND CANNELLONI
Cut the rolled-out sheets of pasta into rectangles, measuring about 10 x 15cm (4 x 6 inches), using a sharp knife or a pastry wheel.

SHAPING RAVIOLI
1 Take a sheet of pasta 10–12cm (4–5 inches) wide. Spoon heaped teaspoons of stuffing at 6cm (2½ inch) intervals along the strip.

2 Using a pastry brush, lightly moisten the edges and between the stuffing with a little water.

3 Lift another sheet of rolled-out pasta over the top and position carefully.

4 Use your fingers to press along the edges of the pasta and between the stuffing to seal.

5 Using a fluted pastry wheel or sharp knife, cut between the stuffing at 6cm (2½ inch) intervals and cut neatly along the long edges.

> TOP TIP
> Until you are confident, it is best not to have large quantities of dough rolled out and drying at one time.

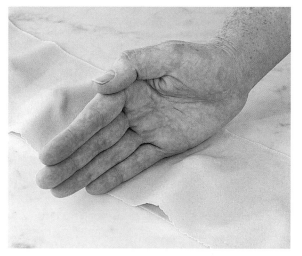

SHAPING RAVIOLINI

1 Take a sheet of pasta. Using a 7.5cm (3 inch) metal fluted round cutter, stamp out circles of dough.

2 Spoon a small heap of stuffing onto each pasta circle. Moisten the edges with a little water.

3 Fold each filled pasta circle in half to give a semi-circular shape, enclosing the filling. Press the edges together lightly to seal.

BEST PASTA SAUCES

FRESH TOMATO SAUCE

Serves 4
Preparation: 10 minutes
Cooking time: about 1 hour
Freezing: suitable
105 cals per serving

900g (2lb) vine-ripened tomatoes, roughly chopped

30ml (2 tbsp) extra-virgin olive oil

2 garlic cloves, peeled and crushed

grated rind of 1 lemon

5ml (1 tsp) dried oregano

30ml (2 tbsp) chopped fresh basil

salt and freshly ground black pepper

pinch of sugar, or to taste (optional)

1 Put the tomatoes, olive oil, garlic, lemon rind and oregano in a saucepan. Bring to the boil, cover and simmer gently for 30 minutes.

2 Add the basil, salt and pepper to taste and a little sugar if required. Simmer, uncovered, for a further 20–30 minutes until the sauce is thickened. If a smooth sauce is preferred, pass through a sieve, remembering to scrape any residues off the underside of the sieve.

3 Toss the sauce with freshly cooked pasta to serve. Accompany with freshly grated Parmesan.

> TOP TIP
> During the summer months when tomatoes are plentiful and at their best, make up several quantities of this sauce and freeze for use during the winter when tomatoes are more expensive and tend to lack flavour.

RICH TOMATO SAUCE

Serves 4–6
Preparation: 10–15 minutes
Cooking time: 25–30 minutes
Freezing: suitable
175–115 cals per serving

50g (2oz) butter

1 onion, peeled and finely chopped

2 garlic cloves, peeled and finely chopped

900g (2lb) ripe tomatoes, preferably plum, or 2 x 400g (14oz) cans tomatoes with their juice

45ml (3 tbsp) sun-dried tomato paste (see page 14)

2 oregano sprigs

salt and freshly ground black pepper

1 Melt the butter in a saucepan, add the onion and garlic and cook over a medium–low heat for about 8 minutes while preparing the tomatoes.

2 If using fresh tomatoes, first skin them. Immerse them in a bowl of boiling water for 30 seconds, then drain and refresh under cold running water. Peel away the skins. Quarter the tomatoes, discard the seeds, then roughly chop the flesh. If using canned plum tomatoes, chop them roughly.

3 Add the tomatoes to the onion and garlic mixture together with the sun-dried tomato paste and oregano sprigs. Cook, uncovered, over a low heat for 25–30 minutes, stirring occasionally, until the sauce is thick and pulpy. Discard the oregano and season with salt and pepper to taste.

4 Toss with hot pasta and serve topped with shavings of Parmesan and chopped parsley.

QUICK TOMATO SAUCE

Serves 4
Preparation: 10–15 minutes
Cooking time: 35 minutes
Freezing: not suitable
100 cals per serving

15ml (1 tbsp) olive oil

75g (3oz) onion, peeled and chopped

75g (3oz) celery, chopped

75g (3oz) carrot, peeled and chopped

1 garlic clove, peeled and crushed

2 x 400g (14oz) cans chopped tomatoes

30ml (2 tbsp) tomato purée

150ml (¼ pint) vegetable stock

100ml (3½fl oz) dry red wine

salt and freshly ground black pepper

1 Heat the olive oil in a large saucepan. Add the vegetables and garlic and cook, stirring occasionally, for 5 minutes or until the vegetables are beginning to soften, but not coloured.

2 Stir in the canned tomatoes, tomato purée, stock, wine and seasoning to taste. Simmer, covered, for about 30 minutes, stirring occasionally.

3 If a smooth-textured sauce is required, transfer to a blender or food processor and blend until smooth.

4 Return the sauce to the pan and heat through. Check the seasoning and adjust, if necessary, before tossing with freshly cooked pasta. Serve topped with freshly grated Parmesan.

VARIATIONS
● *Add 1 small, finely diced red chilli with the garlic at stage 1.*
● *Add 125g (4oz) sautéed sliced mushrooms and 30ml (2 tbsp) chopped parsley at the beginning of stage 4.*

SIMPLE BOLOGNESE SAUCE

Serves 4
Preparation: 10 minutes
Cooking time: about 1 hour
Freezing: suitable
340 cals per serving

15ml (1 tbsp) olive oil

1 large onion, peeled and finely chopped

1 carrot, peeled and finely chopped

1 celery stick, finely chopped

1 garlic clove, peeled and crushed

125g (4oz) button mushrooms, chopped

450g (1lb) minced beef

300ml (½ pint) beef stock

300ml (½ pint) dry red or white wine

400g (14oz) can chopped tomatoes

15ml (1 tbsp) tomato purée

10ml (2 tsp) dried oregano

salt and freshly ground black pepper

30ml (2 tbsp) chopped fresh parsley

1 Heat the oil in a frying pan. Add the onion, carrot, celery and garlic, and fry gently for 5 minutes or until softened. Add the mushrooms and fry for 1 minute.

2 Stir in the beef and cook, stirring, over a high heat until browned. Stir in the stock, wine, tomatoes, tomato purée, oregano and seasoning. Bring to the boil, cover and simmer for 1 hour or until the meat is tender and the sauce is well reduced.

3 Check the seasoning and stir in the parsley before serving with spaghetti, tagliatelle or other pasta. Accompany with freshly grated Parmesan.

CLASSIC BEEF RAGU

Serves 4–6
Preparation: 20 minutes, plus soaking
Cooking time: about 1 hour
Freezing: suitable
655–435 cals per serving

10g (⅓oz) dried porcini mushrooms

15ml (1 tbsp) olive oil

275g (10oz) onion, peeled and finely chopped

75g (3oz) carrot, peeled and finely chopped

75g (3oz) celery, finely chopped

125g (4oz) brown-cap or large button mushrooms, chopped

2 garlic cloves, peeled and crushed

125g (4oz) rindless streaky bacon, chopped

450g (1lb) minced beef

300ml (½ pint) dry white wine

300ml (½ pint) stock

15ml (1 tbsp) tomato purée

10ml (2 tsp) dried oregano

125g (4oz) chicken livers, trimmed and chopped

90ml (6 tsp) double cream

30ml (2 tbsp) chopped fresh parsley

salt and freshly ground black pepper

1 Put the dried porcini mushrooms in a bowl, pour on 100ml (3½fl oz) water and leave to soak for about 30 minutes.

2 Heat the oil in a frying pan. Add the onion, carrot and celery and fry gently for 5 minutes, or until softened. Add the fresh mushrooms and garlic; fry for 1 minute.

3 Add the bacon and beef; cook, stirring, over a high heat until browned. Stir in the wine, stock, tomato purée and oregano. Bring to the boil, cover and simmer for 45 minutes.

4 Stir in the dried mushrooms with their liquor, and the chicken livers. Simmer, uncovered, for 7–10 minutes, until the livers are cooked and the liquid is reduced by half. Add the cream and parsley and allow to bubble for 1 minute.

5 Check the seasoning, before serving with spaghetti, tagliatelle or other pasta of your choice. Accompany with freshly grated Parmesan cheese.

PESTO

Serves 4
Preparation: 10–15 minutes
Freezing: not suitable
380 cals per serving

50g (2oz) fresh basil leaves, roughly chopped

2 garlic cloves, peeled

30ml (2 tbsp) pine nuts, toasted

120ml (4fl oz) extra-virgin olive oil

salt and freshly ground black pepper

50g (2oz) Parmesan cheese, freshly grated

squeeze of lemon juice (optional)

1 Put the basil, garlic and pinenuts in a mortar with a little of the oil and pound with a pestle to a paste. Alternatively, work in a food processor to a fairly smooth paste.

2 Work in the rest of the oil and season with salt and pepper to taste.

3 Transfer to a bowl and fold in the cheese. Check the seasoning and add a squeeze of lemon juice, if desired.

4 Store for up to 2 weeks in the refrigerator in a screw-topped jar, covered with a thin layer of oil.

VARIATION
To make chilli pesto, add 2 seeded and chopped chillis at stage 1, and omit the Parmesan cheese.

ROCKET PESTO

Serves 4
Preparation: 10–15 minutes
Freezing: not suitable
215 cals per serving

50g (2oz) rocket, roughly chopped

1 garlic clove, peeled

15ml (1 tbsp) capers, rinsed and drained

15ml (1 tbsp) chopped fresh parsley

15g (½oz) pine nuts, toasted

15g (½oz) pecorino or Parmesan cheese, freshly grated

75ml (5 tbsp) extra-virgin olive oil

salt and freshly ground black pepper

1 Put the rocket in a mortar, grinder or food processor with the garlic, capers, parsley, pine nuts and cheese. Work to a fairly smooth paste.

2 Stir in the oil and season with salt and pepper to taste.

3 Store, covered with a thin layer of oil, in a screw-topped jar in the refrigerator for up to 2 weeks.

BEST CLASSIC PASTA DISHES

SPAGHETTI WITH CLAMS

Serves 4–6
Preparation: 15 minutes
Cooking time: about 8 minutes
Freezing: not suitable
685–460 cals per serving

700g (1½lb) venus or baby clams in shells

3 garlic cloves

2.5ml (½ tsp) dried chilli flakes

350g (12oz) plum tomatoes (or other flavourful tomatoes)

75ml (5 tbsp) extra-virgin olive oil

100ml (3½fl oz) dry white wine

salt and freshly ground black pepper

400g (14oz) dried spaghetti

30ml (2 tbsp) chopped fresh parsley

40g (1½oz) butter

1 Wash the clams in plenty of cold water and scrub the shells with a small brush. Leave to soak in a bowl of fresh cold water for 10 minutes, then rinse again and drain well. Discard any clams which do not close when their shells are tapped firmly.

2 Finely chop the garlic cloves and crush the chilli flakes; set aside. Immerse the tomatoes in a bowl of boiling water for 30 seconds, then remove with a slotted spoon and peel away their skins. Halve the tomatoes, deseed and chop the flesh.

3 Heat the olive oil in a large frying pan (large enough to hold and toss the spaghetti later). Add the chopped garlic and crushed chilli and cook over a medium-high heat for 2 minutes; do not let the garlic brown. Stir in the chopped tomatoes and wine.

4 Add the clams in their shells to the pan. Season with salt and pepper, stir well and bring to the boil. Cover with a tight-fitting lid and cook for 2–3 minutes to steam open the clams. Remove from the heat and discard any clams which have not opened.

5 Meanwhile, cook the spaghetti in a large pan of boiling salted water until almost ready, but not quite *al dente* (about 1 minute less than the recommended cooking time). Drain thoroughly.

6 Return the clam sauce to the heat and stir in the parsley. Add the drained spaghetti and cook for 1 minute; the pasta should finish its cooking in the clam juices. Add the butter, toss lightly and serve immediately with fresh bread to soak up the last of the sauce.

TOP TIP

If fresh clams are not available, use jars or cans of clams in their shells, available from supermarkets and Italian delicatessens. Drain thoroughly before use.

VARIATIONS
● *Use 1kg (2lb) fresh mussels in their shells instead of the clams. Again, throw away any which remain closed after cooking.*
● *Add a few chopped anchovy fillets to taste.*

CANNELLONI

Serves 6
Preparation: 30 minutes
Cooking time: about 1 hour
Freezing: suitable at end of stage 4
470 cals per serving

about 12 sheets of lasagne

FILLING
20 unpeeled garlic cloves (from 2 garlic bulbs)

30ml (2 tbsp) extra-virgin olive oil

15g (½oz) dried porcini mushrooms

5 shallots, peeled and finely chopped

700g (1½lb) lean minced beef

175ml (6fl oz) red wine

30ml (2 tbsp) chopped fresh thyme

salt and freshly ground black pepper

TOPPING
150ml (¼ pint) single cream

30ml (2 tbsp) sun-dried tomato paste (see page 14)

75g (3oz) provolone or Gruyère cheese, finely grated

1 Preheat the oven to 180°C/350°F/gas 4. To prepare the filling, put the unpeeled but separated garlic cloves in a small roasting tin with 15ml (1 tbsp) of the oil. Toss to coat the garlic in the oil and bake in the oven for 25 minutes until soft. Leave to cool.

2 Meanwhile, put the dried mushrooms in a small bowl and cover with 150ml (¼ pint) boiling water. Leave to soak for 20 minutes, then drain, reserving the liquor. Rinse the mushrooms, then chop finely.

3 Heat the remaining 15ml (1 tbsp) oil in a saucepan. Add the shallots and cook over a medium heat for 5 minutes until soft. Increase the heat and stir in the beef. Cook, stirring frequently to break up the meat, until it is browned. Add the wine, mushrooms and their soaking liquor, and the thyme. Cook over a medium heat for 15–20 minutes or until most of the liquid has evaporated; the mixture should be quite moist.

4 Remove the papery skins from the garlic, then mash lightly with a fork, to give a rough paste. Stir into the beef mixture, season with salt and pepper and set aside.

5 Cook the lasagne sheets in a large saucepan of boiling salted water until *al dente*, or according to the packet instructions. Drain thoroughly in a colander, rinse with cold water and drain again.

6 Lay the lasagne sheets flat on a board or work surface. Spoon the beef mixture along one edge and roll up to enclose the filling. Cut the tubes in half.

7 In a small bowl, mix together the cream and sun-dried tomato paste. Season with pepper. Increase the oven temperature to 200°C/400°F/gas 6.

8 Arrange a layer of cannelloni in the base of a buttered shallow baking dish. Spoon over half of the tomato cream and sprinkle with half of the cheese. Arrange the remaining cannelloni on top and cover with the remaining tomato cream and cheese.

9 Cover the dish with foil and bake in the oven for 10 minutes, then uncover and bake for a further 5–10 minutes until lightly browned and hot. Serve immediately.

TOP TIP
To make the recipe more quickly and simply, use cannelloni tubes that are ready for stuffing and cooking instead of rolling sheets of lasagne.

PASTA PRIMAVERA

Serves 4–6
Preparation: 25 minutes
Cooking time: about 25 minutes
Freezing: not suitable
950–635 cals per serving

175g (6oz) fine asparagus

125g (4oz) sugar snap peas, topped and tailed

1 red pepper

2 celery stalks

2 courgettes

6–8 spring onions, white parts only

225g (8oz) carrots, preferably whole baby ones

1 small onion

50g (2oz) butter

400g (14oz) dried tagliatelle or papardelle

300ml (½ pint) double cream

60ml (4 tbsp) freshly grated Parmesan cheese

salt and freshly ground black pepper

15ml (1 tbsp) oil

20ml (4 tsp) snipped chives

20ml (4 tsp) chopped fresh chervil

20ml (4 tsp) chopped fresh dill

1 Halve the asparagus spears and cook in boiling salted water for 3–4 minutes, adding the sugar snaps after 2 minutes so that both are cooked until just tender. Drain and refresh with cold water, then drain again; set aside.

2 Using a potato peeler, thinly pare the skin from the red pepper and discard, along with the core and seeds. Dice the red pepper, celery, courgettes and spring onions. If the carrots are tiny, baby ones, leave them whole; otherwise peel and cut them into matchsticks. Peel and chop the onion.

3 Melt the butter in a large frying pan. Add the onion and sauté over a medium heat for 7–8 minutes until soft and golden. Add the red pepper and celery and cook for 5 minutes. Stir in the courgettes, carrots and spring onions and cook for 12–15 minutes. stirring frequently, until the vegetables are tender and beginning to colour.

4 Cook the pasta in a large pan of boiling salted water until *al dente*, according to the packet instructions.

5 Meanwhile, stir the cream into the vegetables and bring to a gentle boil. Allow to bubble, stirring frequently for a few minutes until it reduces by about one third. Stir in the asparagus and sugar snaps. Add the Parmesan and heat gently. Season to taste with salt and pepper.

6 Drain the pasta thoroughly and transfer to a warmed large serving bowl. Toss with oil to prevent sticking. Pour the sauce over the pasta and sprinkle with herbs. Toss well and serve at once.

TOP TIP
If you prefer to use another type of pasta, choose a large one, such as rigatoni or cavatappi, which will balance well with the size of the vegetables.

VEGETARIAN LASAGNE

Serves 6
Preparation: about 1 hour
Cooking time: 40 minutes, to bake
Freezing: suitable before baking
685 cals per serving

4 red, orange or yellow peppers

2 medium aubergines

2 onions, peeled

4 garlic cloves, peeled

75ml (5 tbsp) extra-virgin olive oil

75ml (5 tbsp) red wine or water

45ml (3 tbsp) chopped fresh oregano

90ml (6 tbsp) sun-dried tomato paste (see page 14)

salt and freshly ground black pepper

12 sheets dried lasagne

TOPPING
350g (12oz) fresh soft goat's cheese

2 eggs

150ml (¼ pint) single cream

45ml (3 tbsp) dry white breadcrumbs

30ml (2 tbsp) freshly grated Parmesan cheese

1 Preheat the grill to hot. Grill the whole peppers, turning from time to time, until the skins are blackened and blistered all over. This will take about 20 minutes. Allow to cool slightly, then remove the skins (over a bowl to catch the juices). Chop the flesh, discarding the seeds, and set aside with the juices.

2 Meanwhile, cut the aubergines into 1cm (½ inch) dice. Place in a colander, rinse, then sprinkle liberally with salt. Leave for 20 minutes to extract the bitter juices. Rinse again, then blanch in boiling water for 1 minute; drain well.

3 Chop the onions; thinly slice the garlic. Heat the oil in a large saucepan. Add the onions and cook, stirring frequently, for about 8 minutes until soft and golden. Add the garlic and cook for a further 2 minutes. Add the wine and allow to bubble for 1 minute, then stir in the aubergine, oregano and sun-dried tomato paste. Cover and cook over a medium heat for 15–20 minutes, stirring frequently. Remove from the heat and stir in the grilled peppers and seasoning.

4 Preheat the oven to 190°C/375°F/gas 5. Cook the lasagne in a large pan of boiling salted water until *al dente*, or according to the packet instructions. Drain, then drop into a bowl of cold water with 30ml (2 tbsp) oil added to prevent the sheets from sticking. Drain again and lay on a clean tea towel.

5 Oil a baking dish, measuring about 25 x 18 x 8 cm (10 x 7 x 3½ inches). Spread one-third of the filling in the base and then cover with a layer of pasta, trimming to fit the dish as necessary. Add another third of the filling and cover with pasta as before. Cover with the last of the filling and arrange the remaining pasta sheets on top.

6 To make the topping, place the goat's cheese in a bowl, add the eggs and beat well. Stir in the cream and seasoning. Pour over the lasagne and spread evenly. Sprinkle with the breadcrumbs and Parmesan, then bake for about 35–40 minutes or until heated through and lightly browned on top.

TOP TIP
Trim the pasta sheets to fit into the baking dish as necessary.

VARIATION
Replace the goat's cheese topping with 350g (12oz) mozzarella, cut into slices.

SPAGHETTI ALLA CARBONARA

Serves 4–6
Preparation: about 15 minutes
Cooking time: about 7 minutes
Freezing: not suitable
675–450 cals per serving

125–150g (4–5oz) smoked pancetta, in slices

1 garlic clove, peeled

30ml (2 tbsp) extra-virgin olive oil

25g (1oz) butter

3 eggs

30ml (2 tbsp) chopped fresh parsley

30ml (2 tbsp) dry white wine

40g (1½oz) Parmesan cheese, grated

40g (1½oz) pecorino cheese, grated

salt and freshly ground black pepper

400g (14oz) spaghetti

1 Remove the rind from the pancetta, then cut into tiny strips. Halve the garlic. Heat the oil and butter in a heavy-based pan. Add the pancetta and garlic and cook over a medium heat for 3–4 minutes until the pancetta begins to crisp. Turn off the heat; discard the garlic.

2 Meanwhile, in a mixing bowl large enough to hold the cooked spaghetti later, beat the eggs with the parsley, wine and half of each of the cheeses. Season with salt and pepper.

3 Cook the spaghetti in a large pan of boiling salted water until *al dente*, or according to the packet instructions.

4 When the spaghetti is almost cooked, gently reheat the pancetta in the pan. Drain the spaghetti thoroughly, then immediately add to the egg mixture in the bowl with the pancetta. Toss well to cook the eggs until they are creamy. Add the remaining cheeses, toss lightly and serve at once.

TOP TIP
If smoked pancetta (which is usually obtainable from Italian delicatessens) is not available, use 175–225g (6–8oz) smoked bacon instead.

FRESH PASTA WITH ASPARAGUS AND PARMESAN

Serves 4

Preparation: about 30 minutes, plus resting

Cooking time: 6–8 minutes

Freezing: not suitable

585 cals per serving

1 quantity basic pasta dough (see page 12)

225g (8oz) asparagus, trimmed

125g (4oz) unsalted butter

2 garlic cloves, peeled and sliced

60ml (4 tbsp) chopped fresh parsley

50g (2oz) freshly grated Parmesan cheese

freshly ground black pepper

1 Make the pasta; after it has rested for about 30 minutes in the refrigerator, cut the sheets into tagliatelle (see page 17). As you cut each sheet, curl each group of noodles into 'nests' and place on a floured tea towel.

2 To assemble the dish, bring a large saucepan of water to the boil. At the same time, steam the asparagus for 3 minutes until just tender; drain and cut into 5cm (2 inch) lengths. Meanwhile, heat the butter with the garlic in a small pan and cook over a medium heat until it starts to turn brown. Immediately remove from the heat.

3 Add 10ml (2 tsp) salt to the boiling pasta water. Plunge in the noodles, return to the boil and cook for 2–3 minutes until *al dente*. Immediately drain and return the pasta to the pan. Add the asparagus, parsley, butter and half the Parmesan, and toss gently.

4 Serve at once, topped with the remaining Parmesan and plenty of black pepper.

PASTA SICILIANA

Serves 6
Preparation: 30 minutes
Cooking time: 40 minutes
Freezing: not suitable
840 cals per serving

50g (2oz) raisins

50g (2oz) sultanas

90ml (6 tbsp) olive oil

2 fennel bulbs, roughly chopped

175g (6oz) shallots or onions, peeled and roughly chopped

2 x 400g (14oz) cans chopped tomatoes

4 garlic cloves, peeled and crushed

150ml (¼ pint) red wine

150ml (¼ pint) vegetable stock

45ml (3 tbsp) tomato purée

15ml (1 tbsp) caster sugar

salt and freshly ground black pepper

12 fresh sardines, cleaned and filleted

lemon juice and olive oil, for basting

275g (10oz) bucatini or spaghetti

125g (4oz) pine nuts

125g (4oz) fresh white breadcrumbs

30ml (2 tbsp) chopped fresh parsley, plus extra sprigs, to garnish

lemon wedges, to garnish

1 Soak the raisins and sultanas in just enough water to cover for about 1 hour, then drain.

2 Heat 30ml (2 tbsp) olive oil in a large, heavy-based saucepan. Add the fennel and shallots and cook gently for about 5 minutes, stirring frequently. Add the chopped tomatoes and half of the garlic. Slowly bring to the boil, then simmer gently for about 10 minutes. Add the raisins and sultanas, then the wine, stock, tomato purée, sugar and seasoning. Simmer for 30 minutes, stirring occasionally.

3 In the meantime, preheat the grill. Lay the sardines on the grill rack and drizzle over a little lemon juice and olive oil. Grill for about 5 minutes each side, basting frequently.

4 Meanwhile, cook the bucatini or spaghetti in a large pan of boiling salted water until *al dente*, or according to the packet instructions. At the same time, heat the remaining oil in a frying pan. Add the pine nuts and fry until they are just beginning to colour. Add the remaining garlic and breadcrumbs. Fry, stirring, until the breadcrumbs begin to crisp and turn golden brown. Toss in the parsley.

5 Drain the pasta thoroughly and return to the pan. Add the tomato sauce and toss to mix. Spoon into a large serving dish and sprinkle with the breadcrumb mixture. Garnish the grilled sardines with lemon wedges and parsley, and serve with the pasta.

TOP TIP
Bucatini (long, hollow pasta slightly thicker than spaghetti) is traditionally used for this recipe but, if unobtainable, spaghetti makes a good substitute.

SPAGHETTI WITH SPICED MEATBALLS

Serves 4
Preparation: 30 minutes
Cooking time: 20 minutes
Freezing: suitable at end of stage 4.
Defrost the meatballs in sauce
thoroughly before reheating to serve.
965 cals per serving

MEATBALLS
350g (12oz) shoulder of pork

175g (6oz) piece of gammon

175g (6oz) belly of pork

2 garlic cloves, peeled

5ml (1 tsp) coarse sea salt

5ml (1 tsp) granulated sugar

15ml (1 tbsp) coarsely crushed
black pepper

5ml (1 tsp) fennel seeds

1.25ml (¼ tsp) dried chilli flakes

TO FINISH
30ml (2 tbsp) oil

1 quantity fresh or rich tomato
sauce (see page 22)

450g (1lb) spaghetti

oregano sprigs, to garnish

freshly grated Parmesan cheese,
to serve

1 Trim the shoulder of pork, gammon and belly pork of any skin or connective tissue, then cut into rough chunks. Place the meat in a food processor, add all the remaining ingredients and process until smooth. At this stage the sausage meat is ready to use, but you can cover the bowl and leave it to mature in the refrigerator overnight if preferred.

2 With moist hands, roll the sausage meat into small, even-sized balls.

3 Heat the oil in a frying pan and fry the meatballs, in batches if necessary, until evenly browned. Pour over the tomato sauce, bring to the boil and simmer for 10–15 minutes.

4 Meanwhile, cook the pasta in a large pan of boiling salted water until *al dente*. Drain and toss with the meatballs in tomato sauce. Serve garnished with oregano and topped with Parmesan cheese.

> *VARIATION*
> *For a quicker version, replace the meats with 450g (1lb) minced pork and 225g (8oz) unsmoked streaky bacon, finely chopped.*

LAMB AND SPINACH LASAGNE

Serves 6
Preparation: about 45 minutes
Cooking time: about 1 hour 40 minutes
Freezing: not suitable
648 cals per serving

450g (1lb) fresh spinach, washed, or 225g (8oz) frozen spinach

30ml (2 tbsp) vegetable oil

1 onion, peeled and chopped

450g (1lb) minced lamb

225g (8oz) can chopped tomatoes

1 garlic clove, peeled and crushed

30ml (2 tbsp) chopped fresh mint

5ml (1 tsp) ground cinnamon

freshly grated nutmeg

salt and freshly ground black pepper

50g (2oz) butter or margarine

50g (2oz) plain flour

900ml (1½ pints) milk

150ml (5fl oz) natural yogurt

12–15 sheets pre-cooked lasagne

175g (6oz) Cheddar cheese, grated

tomato and chive salad, to serve

1 Place the spinach in a saucepan without any water, cover and cook gently for about 4 minutes or until tender, or thaw if using frozen spinach. Drain well and chop finely.

2 Heat the oil in a large saucepan, add the onion and fry gently for 5 minutes. Add the lamb and brown well, then drain off all the fat.

3 Stir in the spinach with the tomatoes and their juice, the garlic, the mint and the cinnamon. Season with nutmeg, salt and pepper to taste. Bring to the boil and simmer, uncovered, for about 30 minutes. Leave to cool while making the sauce.

4 Preheat the oven to 180°C/350°F/gas 4. Melt the butter in a saucepan, add the flour and cook gently, stirring, for 1–2 minutes. Remove from the heat and gradually blend in the milk. Bring to the boil, stirring constantly, then simmer for 3 minutes until thick and smooth. Add the yogurt and season with salt and pepper to taste.

5 Spoon one-third of the meat mixture over the base of a rectangular baking dish. Cover with 4–5 sheets of lasagne and spread one-third of the white sauce over. Repeat these layers twice more, finishing with the sauce. Sprinkle the cheese on top.

6 Stand the dish on a baking tray. Bake for 45–50 minutes, or until the top is well browned. Serve immediately straight from the baking dish accompanied by a simple salad of sliced tomatoes sprinkled with chopped chives.

PASTA AND MUSHROOMS BAKED WITH TWO CHEESES

Serves 2–3
Preparation: about 20 minutes
Cooking time: about 30 minutes
Freezing: not suitable
826–551 cals per serving

225g (8oz) dried tagliatelle

25g (1oz) butter

1 garlic clove, peeled and crushed

225g (8oz) mushrooms, wiped and thinly sliced

50g (2oz) Stilton cheese

60ml (4 tbsp) double cream

salt and freshly ground black pepper

1 egg, lightly beaten

125g (4oz) freshly grated mozzarella cheese

1 Preheat the oven to 180°C/350°/gas 4. Cook the tagliatelle in plenty of boiling salted water until *al dente*, or according to the packet instructions. Drain well.

2 Meanwhile, melt the butter in a large frying pan and cook the garlic and mushrooms, stirring frequently, until just softened. Crumble in the Stilton cheese and cook for 2–3 minutes, stirring continuously. Stir in the cream and season with salt and pepper to taste.

3 Season the tagliatelle with lots of pepper. Mix into the mushroom sauce. Stir in the egg and mix together thoroughly.

4 Place the mixture into a buttered ovenproof serving dish and sprinkle the mozzarella on top. Cover with kitchen foil and bake for 10–15 minutes or until brown and crusty on top. Serve immediately.

SPINACH AND RICOTTA CANNELLONI

Serves 4–6
Preparation: about 45 minutes
Cooking time: about 1¼ hours
Freezing: not suitable
461 cals per serving

60ml (4 tbsp) olive oil

2 small onions, peeled and finely chopped

30ml (2 tbsp) tomato purée

5ml (1 tsp) mild paprika

2 x 400g (14oz) cans chopped tomatoes

pinch of dried oregano

300ml (10fl oz) dry red wine or vegetable stock

large pinch of sugar

salt and freshly ground black pepper

1 garlic clove, peeled and crushed

450g (1lb) frozen leaf spinach, thawed and drained

450g (1lb) ricotta cheese

pinch of freshly grated nutmeg

18 small sheets pre-cooked lasagne

freshly grated Parmesan cheese

chopped fresh parsley, to garnish

1 Heat half the oil in a heavy-based saucepan, and fry half the onion for 5–10 minutes until very soft. Add the tomato purée and paprika and fry for 2–3 minutes.

2 Add the tomatoes, oregano, red wine and sugar, and season with salt and pepper to taste. Simmer for 20 minutes, stirring occasionally.

3 Preheat the oven to 200°C/400°F/gas 6. Heat the remaining oil in a large saucepan and fry the garlic and remaining onion for 5 minutes, stirring all the time. Add the spinach and cook for 2 minutes. Cool slightly. Stir in the ricotta. Season with nutmeg, salt and pepper.

4 Lay the lasagne sheets on a work surface and divide the spinach mixture between them. Roll up the sheets to enclose the filling.

5 Arrange, seam-side down in a single layer, in a greased ovenproof serving dish. Pour the sauce over and sprinkle with Parmesan. Bake for about 30 minutes or until lightly browned. Serve immediately, garnished with chopped parsley.

BEST QUICK PASTA DISHES

FETTUCINE WITH GREEN VEGETABLES AND GOAT'S CHEESE

Serves 4
Preparation: 10 minutes
Cooking time: about 10 minutes
Freezing: not suitable
465 cals per serving

350g (12oz) baby leeks, or 2 large
leeks, trimmed

75g (3oz) sugar snap peas or
mangetout, trimmed

300g (10oz) fettuccine or
tagliatelle

15g (½oz) butter

30ml (2 tbsp) olive oil

2 garlic cloves, peeled and
crushed

salt and freshly ground black
pepper

1ml (¼ tsp) freshly grated nutmeg

5ml (1 tsp) chopped fresh thyme

175g (6oz) firm goat's cheese, rind
removed

45ml (3 tbsp) capers, rinsed

coarsely chopped flat-leafed
parsley, to garnish

1 Wash the leeks well, then halve each one lengthways. If using large leeks, cut lengthways into long thin ribbons, then across into 7.5cm (3 inch) strips. Cut the sugar snap peas or mangetout in half lengthways.

2 Cook the pasta in a large saucepan of boiling water until *al dente*, or according to the packet instructions.

3 Meanwhile, heat the butter and 15ml (1 tbsp) of the olive oil in a frying pan. Add the leeks, garlic, seasoning and nutmeg and sauté gently for 3–5 minutes until the leeks are softened but still retain a little texture. Add the sugar snap peas or mangetout and thyme and cook for a further 30 seconds.

4 Lightly drain the pasta so that some of the water still clings to it, then return to the saucepan. Stir in the leek mixture, then crumble the cheese on top. Scatter with the capers and fold together lightly. Turn onto serving plates and drizzle with the remaining olive oil. Serve immediately, garnished with chopped parsley.

OLIVE TAGLIATELLE WITH PESTO TRAPANESE

Serves 4
Preparation: 20 minutes, plus resting
Cooking time: 2–3 minutes
Freezing: not suitable
565 cals per serving

1 quantity olive pasta dough
made with 45ml (3 tbsp) black
olive paste (see pages 12–14)

PESTO TRAPENESE
3 ripe tomatoes

4 garlic cloves, peeled

salt and freshly ground black
pepper

50g (2oz) fresh basil leaves

125g (4oz) blanched almonds

150ml (¼ pint) olive oil

TO GARNISH
basil leaves

1 Make the pasta dough. Wrap in cling film and leave it to rest in the refrigerator for at least 30 minutes before attempting to roll out. The pasta will be much more elastic after resting.

2 Meanwhile, make the pesto. Place all the ingredients in a food processor or blender and blend until smooth. Transfer half the pesto to a bowl and set aside. It isn't practical to make a smaller quantity of pesto, so spoon the rest into a jar, cover with a layer of olive oil, and seal. It can be stored in the refrigerator for up to a week.

3 To assemble the dish, roll out the pasta as thinly as possible, using a pasta machine if you have one (see pages 14–16). Then cut the sheets into tagliatelle using the relevant cutters on your pasta machine, or by hand (see page 17).

4 Cook the tagliatelle in a large saucepan of boiling water until *al dente*, or according to the packet instructions. Drain well and toss with the pesto. Serve immediately, garnished with basil leaves.

VARIATION
Serve the pesto with plain egg pasta (see page 12) rather than olive pasta.

CALABRIAN PASTA

Serves 4–6
Preparation: 10 minutes
Cooking time: 12–15 minutes
Freezing: fresh breadcrumbs can be frozen and fried straight from the freezer
695–465 cals per serving

150g (5oz) broccoli

50g (2oz) sultanas

300–350g (10–12oz) ziti, long fusilli or spaghetti

salt and freshly ground black pepper

2 garlic cloves

125ml (4fl oz) olive oil

75g (3oz) white breadcrumbs

25g pine nuts

10ml (2 tsp) anchovy essence or anchovy paste

45ml (3 tbsp) chopped fresh parsley

cayenne pepper, to taste

1 Bring about 600ml (1 pint) water to the boil. Meanwhile, break the broccoli into small florets, cutting the stems into pieces about the same size; place in a saucepan. Put the sultanas in a bowl, pour on a little of the boiling water and leave to soak. Pour the rest of the boiling water over the broccoli, bring to the boil and simmer for 30 seconds; drain.

2 Cook the pasta in a large pan of boiling salted water until *al dente*. Meanwhile, peel and finely chop the garlic. Heat the oil in a frying pan and add the breadcrumbs. Fry, stirring until they begin to crisp, then add the garlic and pine nuts. Continue to fry, stirring, until the pine nuts begin to colour, then add the broccoli. Stir over the heat until the broccoli is thoroughly hot.

3 Drain the pasta in a colander, setting it back on top of the saucepan to catch the last 15ml (1 tbsp) cooking water. Stir the anchovy essence or paste and drained sultanas into this liquid, then return the pasta to the pan. Toss with a generous grinding of black pepper and half of the chopped parsley. Transfer to a heated serving bowl.

4 Mix the remaining parsley into the crumb mixture and sprinkle over the pasta. Sprinkle with cayenne pepper and toss the pasta well at the table.

TOP TIP
Tossing pasta with a little of its cooking water helps to keep the pasta hot, as well as preventing it from drying out.

PASTA AND COURGETTES IN TOMATO CREAM

Serves 4
Preparation: 10 minutes
Cooking time: 10–12 minutes
Freezing: not suitable
570 cals per serving

225g (8oz) courgettes

225g (8oz) tomatoes

350g (12oz) trenette, linguine, fettucine or other pasta

salt and freshly ground black pepper

25g (1oz) butter

150ml (¼ pint) double cream

30ml (2 tbsp) finely grated Parmesan cheese

small handful of fresh basil leaves (roughly torn, if large)

1 Using a swivel vegetable peeler, pare strips lengthways from the courgettes to make ribbons, discarding the outside skin pieces; set aside. Immerse the tomatoes in a bowl of boiling water for 30 seconds, then drain and peel away the skins. Roughly chop the tomato flesh.

2 Cook the pasta in a large pan of boiling salted water until *al dente*. Meanwhile, melt the butter in a pan, add the chopped tomatoes and cook gently until softened. Add the cream and season with salt and pepper. Gently stir in the courgette ribbons and simmer for about 2 minutes, until they are just soft.

3 Drain the pasta and transfer to a warmed serving bowl. Pour the sauce over the pasta and sprinkle on half of the Parmesan. Toss very gently to mix. Scatter with the remaining Parmesan and basil leaves and serve immediately.

VARIATION
Use long thin strips of leek instead of the courgettes. Add them to the pasta for the last 2 minutes of its cooking. Drain together with the pasta and toss in the tomato cream.

PASTA WITH MUSSELS AND RED PESTO

Serves 4–6
Preparation: 20 minutes
Cooking time: about 10 minutes
Freezing: not suitable
895–595 cals per serving

1kg (2lb) mussels in shells

1 shallot or small onion

90ml (3fl oz) dry white wine

30ml (2 tbsp) chopped fresh parsley

400g (14oz) dried ribbon pasta, such as tagliatelle

40g (1½oz) butter

RED PESTO
2 garlic cloves, peeled

25g (1oz) walnuts

40g (1½oz) basil leaves (from 3 basil plants)

60ml (4 tbsp) finely chopped sun-dried tomatoes in oil

75ml (5 tbsp) extra-virgin olive oil

30ml (2 tbsp) pine nuts

75ml (5 tbsp) freshly grated Parmesan cheese

salt and freshly ground black pepper

TO SERVE
30ml (2 tbsp) finely grated Parmesan cheese

1 First make the red pesto: roughly chop the garlic cloves and walnuts. Put them into a food processor or blender with the basil leaves, chopped sun-dried tomatoes plus 30ml (2 tbsp) of their oil, the olive oil and pine nuts. Process until fairly smooth and creamy.

2 Transfer the paste to a bowl and stir in the grated Parmesan. Season with a little salt (the sun-dried tomatoes and the cheese are both already quite salty) and lots of pepper. Set aside.

3 Wash the mussels thoroughly in plenty of cold water, scrubbing the shells, and remove the beards. Discard any mussels which do not close when tapped firmly. Drain well. Peel and chop the shallot or onion.

4 Place the mussels in a large saucepan with the shallot or onion, wine and parsley. Season lightly. Cook over a high heat until the liquid comes to the boil, then cover with a tight-fitting lid and cook for 3–4 minutes until the mussels are steamed open. Drain the mussels and discard any which have not opened.

5 Remove most of the mussels from their shells, then put all of them into a bowl and set aside. Meanwhile, cook the pasta in a large saucepan of boiling water until *al dente*, or according to the packet instructions. Drain well.

6 To serve, transfer the red pesto to a large saucepan. Warm gently on a low heat. Add the mussels to the pan and heat very gently. Remove from the heat and stir in the butter. Add the pasta to the pan and toss to mix. Serve immediately, with freshly grated Parmesan.

TOP TIP
You can prepare the red pesto up to a week in advance and store it in a jar, topped with a layer of oil to seal in the flavours.

LONG FUSILLI WITH ASPARAGUS AND PARMESAN

Serves 4–6
Preparation: 5 minutes
Cooking time: 12 minutes
Freezing: not suitable
875–585 cals per serving

400g (14oz) thin asparagus

1 onion

salt and freshly ground black pepper

50g (2oz) butter

90ml (3fl oz) dry white wine

400g (14oz) dried long fusilli, tagliatelle or penne

300ml (½ pint) extra-thick double cream

50g (2oz) Parmesan cheese, freshly grated

1 Trim the asparagus, discarding any tough woody bases. Pare any larger stalks with a vegetable peeler, otherwise leave whole. Peel and finely chop the onion.

2 Pour sufficient water into a frying pan to give a 2cm (³/₄ inch) depth. Add a pinch of salt and bring to the boil. Add the asparagus spears and cook for 4–5 minutes until almost tender. Drain, reserving 75ml (5 tbsp) of the cooking water. Cut the asparagus into 5cm (2 inch) lengths and set aside.

3 Melt the butter in the frying pan. Add the onion and cook over a medium heat for about 5 minutes until softened and beginning to colour. Stir in the asparagus and cook for 1 minute. Pour in the reserved cooking water and the wine. Cook over a high heat until almost all the liquid has evaporated.

4 Meanwhile, cook the pasta in a large pan of boiling salted water until *al dente*, or according to the packet instructions

5 Add the cream to the sauce and stir well. Heat until bubbling. Stir in half of the grated Parmesan and salt and pepper to taste.

6 Drain the pasta thoroughly and add to the sauce. Toss well to mix. Serve at once, sprinkled with the remaining Parmesan and pepper to taste.

TOP TIP
Try to use pencil-thin asparagus, as larger stalks require peeling and, of course, yield fewer tender pieces of asparagus.

TAGLIATELLE WITH SAGE, PIMENTO AND GARLIC

Serves 4–6
Preparation: 10 minutes
Cooking time: about 10 minutes
Freezing: not suitable
775–520 cals per serving

1 small onion

2 garlic cloves

60ml (4 tbsp) extra-virgin olive oil

400g (14oz) can pimento in brine

30ml (2 tbsp) chopped fresh sage

150ml (¼ pint) extra-thick double cream

75ml (5 tbsp) freshly grated Parmesan cheese

salt and freshly ground black pepper

400g (14oz) green and plain tagliatelle

sage sprigs, to garnish

1 Peel and finely chop the onion and garlic. Heat the oil in a large frying pan. Add the onion and garlic and cook over a medium heat for about 5 minutes until softened; do not allow to brown.

2 Drain and rinse the canned pimento then drain well and cut into fairly small dice. Add to the frying pan with the chopped sage and continue cooking for 3 minutes. Stir in the cream and bring to a simmer, then stir in all but 15ml (1 tbsp) of the grated Parmesan. Season with salt and pepper to taste.

3 Meanwhile, cook the pasta in a large pan of boiling water until *al dente*, or according to the packet instructions. Fresh pasta will require only 2–3 minutes.

4 To serve, drain the pasta thoroughly and add to the sauce. Toss well to mix. Serve sprinkled with the remaining grated Parmesan and garnished with sage leaves.

TOP TIP

If you prefer to use ordinary double cream, increase the quantity by about one-third and reduce the creamy sauce slightly by simmering until the desired consistency is obtained.

VARIATION

Use pasta tubes, such as rigatoni or penne, in place of the tagliatelle and add 175g (6oz) diced mozzarella cheese to the sauce at the end of cooking. The cheese cubes should melt softly when tossed in the pasta but not disappear completely into the sauce.

PAPARDELLE WITH ARTICHOKES AND CREAM

Serves 4–6
Preparation: 5–10 minutes
Cooking time: 10 minutes
Freezing: not suitable
835–555 cals per serving

400g (14oz) dried papardelle or tagliatelle

12 artichoke hearts, preserved in oil

2 garlic cloves, peeled

25g (1oz) butter

45ml (3 tbsp) chopped fresh parsley

300ml (½ pint) extra-thick double cream

90ml (6 tbsp) freshly grated pecorino or Parmesan cheese

salt and freshly ground black pepper

1 Cook the pasta in a large pan of boiling salted water until *al dente*, or according to the packet instructions.

2 Meanwhile, prepare the sauce. Drain the artichoke hearts and slice them thinly. Finely chop the garlic. Melt the butter in a large frying pan. Add the garlic and cook over a gentle heat for about 3 minutes to soften; do not allow to brown.

3 Add the artichokes and 30ml (2 tbsp) of the chopped parsley to the frying pan. Cook, stirring, for 2 minutes. Stir in the cream and bring to a simmer. Stir in the grated cheese and cook for a further 1 minute. Season with salt and pepper to taste.

4 To serve, drain the pasta thoroughly in a colander. Add to the sauce and toss well to mix. Serve at once, sprinkled with the remaining chopped parsley.

> TOP TIP
> Artichoke hearts in oil are available from many supermarkets and from Italian delicatessens. They have a much better flavour than canned artichoke hearts in brine.

> *VARIATION*
> *Add 50–75g (2–3oz) roughly chopped walnuts to the sauce at the same stage as the pecorino or Parmesan cheese. If available, use 45ml (3 tbsp) walnut oil in place of the butter.*

PENNE WITH OLIVES, ANCHOVIES AND CHILLI

Serves 4-6
Preparation: 8–10 minutes
Cooking time: about 10 minutes
Freezing: not suitable
660–440 cals per serving

400g (14oz) dried penne

2 garlic cloves

50g (2oz) can anchovies in olive oil

2.5ml (½ tsp) dried chilli flakes

30ml (2 tbsp) chopped fresh parsley

225g (8oz) stoned mixed black and green olives

60ml (4 tbsp) extra-virgin olive oil

30–45ml (2–3 tbsp) freshly grated Parmesan cheese, plus extra to serve

1 Bring a large saucepan of salted water to the boil. Add the pasta and cook until *al dente*, or according to the packet instructions.

2 Meanwhile, peel and thinly slice the garlic cloves. Place in a saucepan with the anchovies and their oil. Add the chilli flakes and cook over a fairly high heat for 2–3 minutes, stirring to break up the anchovies with a wooden spoon; do not allow the garlic to brown. Stir in the parsley and remove from the heat.

3 Transfer the contents of the pan to a food processor and add the olives and olive oil. Process for a few seconds to give a coarse paste. Season with pepper to taste.

4 When the pasta is cooked, drain thoroughly in a colander. Return to the saucepan and add the pounded olive mixture and freshly grated Parmesan. Toss well to coat the pasta. Serve immediately, topped with Parmesan shavings, and accompanied by a crisp leafy salad.

TOP TIP
You probably won't need to add salt to this recipe as the ingredients themselves are naturally salty.

VARIATION
Add some steamed broccoli or cauliflower florets to the pasta and sauce with the grated Parmesan.

PASTA WITH PRAWNS, GARLIC AND SPINACH

Serves 4
Preparation: 5 minutes
Cooking time: 10 minutes
Freezing: not suitable
610 cals per serving

350g (12oz) spaghetti

salt and freshly ground black pepper

125g (4oz) butter

2 garlic cloves, peeled and crushed

225g (8oz) cooked peeled prawns

225g (8oz) spinach leaves, trimmed and chopped

30–45ml (2–3 tbsp) chopped fresh parsley

1 Cook the spaghetti in a large saucepan of boiling salted water until *al dente*, or according to the packet instructions.

2 Meanwhile, in a large saucepan, melt the butter with the garlic; do not allow the garlic to brown. Then add the prawns and turn to coat with the butter. Heat through gently for 1 minute only.

3 When the spaghetti is cooked, drain it thoroughly and return it to the pan. Add the spinach, buttered prawns and parsley. Season liberally with salt and pepper and toss well over the heat until the spinach wilts. Serve immediately.

TOP TIP
To save time, use a bag of ready-prepared spinach leaves, available from most supermarkets.

ORECCHIETTE WITH ROCKET AND CHERRY TOMATOES

Serves 4

Preparation: 10 minutes

Cooking time: about 10 minutes

Freezing: not suitable

580 cals per serving

400g (14oz) dried orecchiette

salt and freshly ground black pepper

45ml (3 tbsp) olive oil

30ml (2 tbsp) pine nuts

450g (1lb) very ripe cherry tomatoes, halved

75g (3oz) rocket leaves

50g (2oz) Parmesan cheese, freshly pared, to serve

1 Cook the pasta in a large saucepan of boiling salted water until *al dente*, or according to the packet instructions.

2 A few minutes before the pasta will be ready, heat 30ml (2 tbsp) of the oil in a large saucepan. Add the pine nuts and cook for 1–2 minutes until golden. Add the tomatoes and cook for barely 1 minute until only just heated through, not disintegrated.

3 Drain the pasta thoroughly and toss with the remaining olive oil. Add the pasta to the tomatoes, then add the rocket. Carefully stir to mix and heat through. Season generously with salt and pepper. Serve immediately, topped with plenty of Parmesan shavings.

VARIATION
Use young spinach leaves in place of the rocket.

LINGUINE WITH PARMA HAM AND SUN-DRIED TOMATOES

Serves 4–6
Preparation: 5 minutes
Cooking time: 10 minutes
Freezing: not suitable
1020–680 cals per serving

400g (14oz) dried linguine or
fettucine

salt and freshly ground black
pepper

30ml (2 tbsp) olive oil

125g (4oz) Parma ham, cut into
thin strips

65g (2½oz) butter

1 large onion, peeled and
chopped

2 garlic cloves, peeled and
crushed

50g (2oz) sun-dried tomatoes,
drained and cut into strips

150ml (¼ pint) double cream

150g (5oz) mascarpone cheese

15–30ml (1–2 tbsp) chopped fresh
marjoram or oregano

30–40ml (2–3 tbsp) toasted pine
nuts (optional)

1 Cook the pasta in a large saucepan of boiling salted water until *al dente*, or according to the packet instructions.

2 Meanwhile, heat the oil in a frying pan, add the Parma ham strips and fry quickly for about 1 minute or until frazzled. Using a slotted spoon, remove the ham from the pan and set aside.

3 Add the butter to the frying pan and gently fry the onion, garlic and sun-dried tomatoes for 2 minutes.

4 In a saucepan, gently heat the cream with the mascarpone, stirring until smooth. Season with salt and pepper.

5 Drain the pasta and, while still hot, add to the frying pan and toss to mix. Add the cream mixture, together with half of the Parma ham and half the marjoram or oregano. Toss to mix.

6 Serve at once, topped with the remaining Parma ham, herbs and toasted pine nuts, if using.

VARIATIONS
● *Use strips of pancetta or smoked streaky bacon instead of Parma ham and cook in the same way.*
● *Sautéed sliced mushrooms or asparagus tips also make tasty additions.*

LINGUINE WITH CHICKEN LIVERS AND VERMOUTH

Serves 4
Preparation: 10 minutes
Cooking time: 12 minutes
Freezing: not suitable
830 cals per serving

700g (1½lb) chicken livers

400g (14oz) dried linguine

salt and freshly ground black pepper

45ml (3 tbsp) vegetable oil

6 spring onions, trimmed and sliced

5ml (1 tsp) cornflour

150ml (¼ pint) dry vermouth

30ml (2 tbsp) chopped fresh sage

50g (2oz) butter, cubed

sage sprigs, to garnish

1 Trim any fat and white membrane from the chicken livers. Rinse the livers under cold water and pat dry with kitchen paper. Cut into smaller pieces.

2 Cook the pasta in a large saucepan of boiling salted water until *al dente*, or according to the packet instructions.

3 Meanwhile, heat the oil in a frying pan until smoking. Add the spring onions followed by the chicken livers. Fry, stirring, for about 2 minutes until the livers are evenly browned, then sprinkle with the cornflour and stir in. Pour over the vermouth, add the chopped sage, cover and cook for 2 minutes. Season with salt and pepper to taste.

4 Drain the pasta thoroughly, toss with the butter and pile into a warmed serving dish. Pour over the chicken liver sauce and serve immediately, garnished with sage sprigs.

SUMMER PASTA

Serves 2–3
Preparation: 5–10 minutes
Cooking time: about 15 minutes
Freezing: not suitable
636–424 cals per serving

175g (6oz) dried tagliatelle,
spinach and plain mixed, or other
pasta

salt and freshly ground black
pepper

2 good-sized tomatoes, skinned,
seeded and chopped

3–4 anchovy fillets, well drained
and finely chopped

90ml (6 tbsp) single cream

115g (4oz) cooked peeled prawns

200g can mussels in vinegar,
drained and rinsed

1 garlic clove, peeled and crushed

freshly grated Parmesan cheese,
to serve

extra whole prawns in shells and
herb sprigs, to garnish (optional)

1 Cook the pasta in a large saucepan of boiling water until *al dente*, or according to the packet instructions.

2 Meanwhile, place the chopped tomatoes and anchovies in a saucepan with the single cream, prawns, mussels, tomato purée, garlic and seasoning and heat gently, stirring.

3 Drain the pasta well and stir into the sauce. Serve immediately, garnished with whole prawns in their shells and fresh herbs, if wished, and with Parmesan handed around separately.

PORK AND GREEN BEAN PASTA

Serves 4

Preparation: about 15 minutes, plus marinating

Cooking time: 20–25 minutes

Freezing: not suitable

572 cals per serving

450g (1lb) pork, trimmed of fat and cut into thin strips

75g (3oz) streaky bacon, rinded and finely chopped

225g (8oz) onions, preferably red, skinned and finely sliced

15ml (1 tbsp) wholegrain mustard

115ml (4fl oz) dry cider

1 garlic clove, peeled and crushed

45ml (3 tbsp) vegetable oil

salt and freshly ground black pepper

175g (6oz) green beans, topped, tailed and halved

1 red pepper, seeded and cut into strips

75g (3oz) dried pasta shapes

15ml (1 tbsp) soy sauce

60ml (4 tbsp) chicken stock

1 Place the pork, bacon and onions together in a bowl and stir in the mustard, cider, garlic, and 15ml (1 tbsp) of the oil. Season well with salt and pepper and stir to mix. Cover and refrigerate overnight. Allow at least 8 hours marinating time for the flavours to develop.

2 The next day, blanch the green beans and red pepper in boiling salted water for 2 minutes. Drain well, then run under cold water and set aside to cool.

3 Cook the pasta in plenty of boiling salted water for 10–12 minutes, or until *al dente*. Drain well.

4 Meanwhile, drain the meat from the marinade, reserving the juices. Heat the remaining oil in a large frying pan or wok and stir-fry the meat and onions over a high heat for 3–4 minutes until lightly browned.

5 Stir in the beans, pepper and pasta with the marinade, soy sauce, stock and seasoning. Bring to the boil, then simmer for about 5 minutes, stirring occasionally, until piping hot. Adjust the seasoning and serve immediately.

BEST LIGHT LUNCHES

PRAWN, FRESH PEA AND PASTA SALAD

Serves 4
Preparation: 15 minutes
Cooking time: 10 minutes
Freezing: not suitable
510 cals per serving

175g (6oz) dried pasta, such as penne, shells or twists

125g (4oz) shelled fresh peas ie about 450g (1lb) peas in the pod

225g (8oz) large cooked peeled prawns

30ml (2 tbsp) chopped fresh mint

15ml (1 tbsp) chopped fresh chives

DRESSING
60ml (4 tbsp) hazelnut oil

30ml (2 tbsp) vegetable oil

45ml (3 tbsp) freshly squeezed orange juice

15ml (1 tbsp) lemon juice

2.5ml (½ tsp) clear honey

salt and freshly ground black pepper

TO GARNISH
50g (2oz) hazelnuts, toasted

mint sprigs

1 Bring a large pan of lightly salted water to a rolling boil. Add the pasta, return to the boil and cook for 8–10 minutes until barely *al dente*. Drain well and transfer to a large bowl.

2 Meanwhile, prepare the dressing. Place all the ingredients in a screw-topped jar and shake well until evenly combined. As soon as the pasta is cooked, pour over two-thirds of the dressing and toss until well coated. Set aside to cool.

3 Blanch the peas in boiling salted water for 1 minute, then drain, refresh under cold water and pat dry. Dry the prawns and set aside.

4 Assemble the salad just before serving. Add the peas, prawns and herbs to the pasta with the remaining dressing and toss well. Serve at once, topped with the toasted hazelnuts and garnished with mint.

VARIATION
For an enriched version, add 60ml (4 tbsp) mayonnaise or crème fraîche to the pasta along with the dressing.

MEDITERRANEAN PASTA SALAD

Serves 4
Preparation: 15 minutes, plus standing
Cooking time: 2–10 minutes
Freezing: not suitable
415 cals per serving

175g (6oz) fresh or dried pasta shapes

30ml (2 tbsp) extra-virgin olive oil

4 sun-dried tomatoes in oil, drained

4–6 spring onions

225g (8oz) cherry tomatoes

about 8–10 black olives

8–12 basil leaves

DRESSING
2 sun-dried tomatoes in oil, drained

30ml (2 tbsp) oil from the sun-dried tomato jar

30ml (2 tbsp) red wine vinegar

1 garlic clove

15ml (1 tbsp) tomato purée

pinch of sugar (optional)

coarse sea salt and freshly ground black pepper

30ml (2 tbsp) extra-virgin olive oil

1 Cook the pasta in a large pan of boiling salted water with 15ml (1 tbsp) olive oil added until *al dente*. Fresh pasta will only take about 2–3 minutes. For dried pasta, cook according to the packet instructions. Drain the pasta in a colander, then refresh under cold running water. Drain thoroughly and transfer to a large bowl. Stir in 15ml (1 tbsp) olive oil to prevent the pasta from sticking together.

2 Slice the sun-dried tomatoes. Trim and finely shred the spring onions. Halve the cherry tomatoes. Tear the basil leaves into smaller pieces, if preferred.

3 Add the sun-dried and cherry tomatoes, spring onions, olives and basil to the pasta and toss to mix.

4 To make the dressing, put the sun-dried tomatoes (with their oil), vinegar, garlic and tomato purée in a blender or food processor. Add the sugar, if using, and salt and pepper. With the motor running, pour the oil through the feeder tube and process briefly to make a fairly thick dressing.

5 Pour the dressing over the pasta and toss well. Cover and leave to stand to allow the flavours to mingle for 1–2 hours before serving if possible.

TOP TIP
Take extra care to avoid overcooking the pasta and cool it quickly under cold running water to preserve the texture.

VARIATION
Toss cubes of mature Cheddar cheese into the salad and serve with wholemeal bread and a leafy green salad for a more substantial meal.

PASTA SALAD WITH PRAWNS, CHILLIES AND BEANS

Serves 4–6
Preparation: 20 minutes, plus infusing
Cooking time: 10 minutes
Freezing: not suitable
670–450 cals per serving

150ml (¼ pint) extra-virgin olive oil

2 whole dried red chillies

2 garlic cloves, peeled and roughly chopped

grated rind and juice of 1 large lemon

350g (12oz) dried pasta twists

salt and freshly ground black pepper

175g (6oz) French beans, halved

450g (1lb) cooked Mediterranean prawns (shelled if preferred)

60ml (4 tbsp) chopped fresh herbs, such as basil, chervil, chives, mint and parsley

50g (2oz) pine nuts, toasted

1 Place the oil, chillies, garlic and grated lemon rind in a small pan and heat gently without boiling for 10 minutes. Remove from the heat and leave to infuse and cool. Strain and reserve the flavoured oil.

2 Cook the pasta in a large pan of lightly salted boiling water for 8–10 minutes or until *al dente*. Drain well and immediately toss with the lemon juice and half of the flavoured oil. Leave to cool at room temperature.

3 Meanwhile, cook the beans in lightly salted boiling water for 3 minutes or until just cooked; drain and immediately refresh under cold water. Pat dry on kitchen paper.

4 Add the prawns, beans and herbs to the cooled pasta and stir well to combine. Add extra flavoured olive oil and seasoning to taste. Serve sprinkled with the pine nuts.

GINGERED PRAWN AND LASAGNETTE SALAD

Serves 4
Preparation: 20 minutes
Cooking time: 15 minutes
Freezing: not suitable
465 cals per serving

450g (1lb) large raw prawns in their shells

225g (8oz) fresh or dried lasagnette

salt and freshly ground black pepper

30ml (2 tbsp) oil

225g (8oz) baby carrots, halved lengthways

125g (4oz) baby courgettes, halved lengthways

1 bunch spring onions, trimmed and sliced

4 garlic cloves, peeled and thinly sliced

1 red chilli, seeded and chopped

175g (6oz) Chinese leaves, shredded

60ml (4 tbsp) roughly chopped fresh parsley or coriander

DRESSING
1 piece preserved stem ginger, finely chopped, plus 30ml (2 tbsp) from the jar

15ml (1 tbsp) soy sauce

15ml (1 tbsp) sesame oil

TO GARNISH
30ml (2 tbsp) sesame seeds, toasted

1 Peel the prawns and butterfly them by snipping each one lengthways almost from head to tail, leaving the tail end intact; set aside.

2 For the dressing, combine the ginger and syrup, soy sauce and sesame oil.

3 Cook the pasta in a large pan of boiling salted water until *al dente*. Drain thoroughly and place in a bowl. Add the dressing and toss to coat evenly.

4 Heat the oil in a large frying pan or wok. Add the carrots and courgettes and fry very quickly over a high heat until lightly charred. Remove with a slotted spoon and set aside. Add the spring onions, garlic, chilli, Chinese leaves and prawns. Fry quickly until the prawns are cooked and the leaves are just wilted.

5 Add all the vegetables to the pasta with the parsley or coriander, and a little seasoning. Serve warm, scattered with toasted sesame seeds.

VARIATION
Instead of raw prawns, use 350g (12oz) cooked peeled prawns. Omit stage 1, add the prawns at the end of stage 4 and heat through briefly.

SMOKED MUSSEL AND PASTA SALAD

Serves 4
Preparation: 15 minutes
Cooking time: 15–20 minutes
Freezing: not suitable
660 cals per serving

2 red peppers

8 salad onions

90ml (3fl oz) olive oil

1 garlic clove

10ml (2 tsp) red wine vinegar

salt and freshly ground black pepper

350g (12oz) dried pasta shapes, such as shells, tubes or bows

125g (4oz) fresh or frozen peas

2 x 105g (3½oz) cans smoked mussels, drained

30ml (2 tbsp) chopped fresh parsley

1 avocado

parsley sprigs, to garnish

1 Cut the peppers into quarters, then remove the core and seeds. Peel the onions and cut into quarters.

2 Preheat the grill. Place the quartered onions and peppers, skin-side up, in the grill pan and drizzle with 15ml (1 tbsp) of the olive oil. Grill until the pepper skins are charred and the onions nicely browned. (You may need to remove the onions before the peppers.) Place the peppers in a bowl and cover with a plate; the steam created will help to loosen the skins.

3 When the peppers are cool enough to handle, peel away the skins. Place half the peppers in a blender or food processor. Peel and roughly chop the garlic; add to the blender with the remaining oil and the vinegar. Work to a purée, and season with salt and pepper to taste.

4 Cook the pasta in a large pan of boiling salted water according to the packet instructions until *al dente*. About 5 minutes before the end of the cooking time, add the peas, then immediately refresh under cold running water. Drain thoroughly.

5 Cut the remaining pepper into strips. Halve the avocado, remove the stone and skin, then cut the flesh into chunks.

6 Transfer the pasta and peas to a large bowl, add the pepper dressing and toss well. Add the pepper strips, grilled onions, mussels, chopped parsley and avocado. Toss gently to combine all the ingredients and check the seasoning. Serve garnished with parsley.

VARIATION
Canned smoked oysters make a delicious alternative to the mussels.

CREAMY HERB PASTA WITH VEGETABLES

Serves 4–6
Preparation: 25 minutes, plus infusing
Cooking time: 10 minutes
Freezing: not suitable
715–475 cals per serving

25g (1oz) mixed fresh herbs, such as basil, chervil, chives, dill and parsley, roughly chopped

5ml (1 tsp) dried oregano

120ml (4 fl oz) extra-virgin olive oil

700g (1½lb) mixed vegetables to include courgettes, asparagus tips, French beans, shelled broad beans, baby carrots, cherry tomatoes

salt and freshly ground black pepper

2 shallots, peeled and finely chopped

1 garlic clove, peeled and finely chopped

400g (14oz) dried tagliatelle

90ml (6 tbsp) single cream

freshly pared Parmesan cheese, to serve

1 Place the fresh herbs and dried oregano a bowl. Add all but 30ml (2 tbsp) of the olive oil. Stir well and set aside for a few hours, if possible, to infuse.

2 Prepare the vegetables. Thinly slice the courgettes; trim the asparagus spears and the French beans; peel the carrots and halve lengthways, if large. Blanch all the vegetables except the tomatoes, separately, in a large pan of lightly salted boiling water. Blanch the courgette slices and asparagus for 1–2 minutes and the beans and carrots for 2–3 minutes. After blanching, drain and immediately pat dry on kitchen paper.

3 Heat the remaining oil in a large frying pan, add the shallots and garlic and sauté for 5 minutes. Add the vegetables to the pan, stir-fry over a gentle heat to heat through, then add the herb mixture.

4 Meanwhile, cook the tagliatelle in a large pan of boiling salted water for 10–12 minutes until *al dente*.

5 Drain the pasta, reserving 60ml (4 tbsp) of the cooking water. Add the pasta and reserved water to the frying pan and toss with the vegetables and sauce. Stir in the cream and heat through briefly. Serve at once, seasoned with salt and pepper. Serve the Parmesan separately.

CHICKEN, PINE NUT AND ROCKET PASTA

Serves 4
Preparation: 10 minutes
Cooking time: about 20 minutes
Freezing: not suitable
480 cals per serving

2 large chicken breasts

salt and freshly ground black pepper

250g (9oz) penne

30ml (2 tbsp) olive oil

1 onion, peeled and thinly sliced

2 garlic cloves, peeled and crushed

40g (1½oz) pine nuts, lightly toasted

125g (4oz) rocket or watercress

15ml (1 tbsp) light brown (muscovado) sugar

15ml (1 tbsp) grainy mustard

15ml (1 tbsp) white wine vinegar

75ml (5 tbsp) Greek yogurt

1 Slice each chicken breast in half horizontally, then cut each piece into three. Season lightly with salt and pepper and place between two layers of cling film. Beat with a rolling pin to flatten.

2 Cook the pasta in a large pan of boiling salted water until *al dente* or according to the packet instructions.

3 Meanwhile, heat the oil in a frying pan. Add the chicken pieces and fry for about 3 minutes on each side until cooked through. Drain and keep warm. Add the onion to the pan and cook gently for 3 minutes until softened. Stir in the garlic and pine nuts and cook for a further 1 minute.

4 Drain the pasta and return to the saucepan. Add the contents of the frying pan, the chicken and the rocket and toss lightly together. Transfer to warmed serving plates.

5 Stir the brown sugar, mustard, vinegar and yogurt into the pan with 100ml (3½fl oz) water. Heat through, stirring, for 1 minute without boiling, then spoon over the pasta and serve immediately.

PASTA WITH COURGETTES AND BALSAMIC VINEGAR

Serves 4–6
Preparation: 10 minutes
Cooking time: 25 minutes
Freezing: not suitable
725–480 cals per serving

450g (1lb) courgettes

1 small onion

2 garlic cloves

75ml (5 tbsp) extra-virgin olive oil

45ml (3 tbsp) pine nuts

45ml (3 tbsp) chopped fresh parsley

salt and freshly ground black pepper

400g (14oz) tagliatelle, papardelle or pasta shapes

15–30ml (1–2 tbsp) balsamic vinegar

90ml (6 tbsp) freshly grated Parmesan or pecorino cheese

1 Cut the courgettes into thin slices. Peel and finely chop the onion and garlic. Heat 30ml (2 tbsp) olive oil in a large frying pan. Add the pine nuts and cook, stirring, over a medium-high heat for 2–3 minutes until lightly browned. Transfer to a small bowl and set aside.

2 Add the remaining 45ml (3 tbsp) oil to the pan. Stir in the onion and garlic and cook over a gentle heat for 2 minutes to soften. Add the courgettes and increase the heat. Cook, stirring, for about 4 minutes until just beginning to brown.

3 Add the parsley, seasoning and 30ml (2 tbsp) water to the pan. Cover, lower the heat and cook gently for 15 minutes, stirring twice.

4 Meanwhile, cook the pasta in a large pan of boiling salted water until *al dente*, or according to the packet instructions. (Fresh pasta ribbons will need only 2–3 minutes' cooking time.)

5 Uncover the courgettes and cook for a moment or two over a high heat, stirring gently, until any excess liquid has evaporated. Remove from the heat and sprinkle with the balsamic vinegar and pine nuts.

6 Drain the pasta thoroughly and add to the courgettes with two-thirds of the grated cheese. Toss to mix. Serve at once, sprinkled with the remaining grated Parmesan or pecorino.

PASTA AND PRAWN SALAD

Serves 6

Preparation: about minutes, plus standing

Cooking time: 10–15 minutes

Freezing: not suitable

181 cals per serving

175g (6oz) dried pasta shells

salt and freshly ground black pepper

150ml (5fl oz) unsweetened apple juice

5ml (1 tsp) chopped fresh mint

5ml (1 tsp) white wine vinegar

225g (8oz) crisp eating apples

225g (8oz) cooked peeled prawns

shredded lettuce leaves, to serve

paprika, to garnish

1 Cook the pasta in a large saucepan of boiling salted water for 10–12 minutes or until *al dente*. Drain well.

2 Whisk together the apple juice, mint and vinegar. Season with salt and pepper to taste.

3 Core and slice the apples. Stir the prawns, apples and pasta into the dressing until well mixed and thoroughly coated. Cover and refrigerate for 2–3 hours.

4 To serve, add the shredded lettuce and toss well. Then dust with a sprinkling of paprika.

PENNE WITH ASPARAGUS AND CHEESE

Serves 6
Preparation: 10–15 minutes
Cooking time: about 15 minutes
Freezing: not suitable
485 cals per serving

SALAD
225g (8oz) dried pasta shapes,
such as quills, shells or spirals

salt and freshly ground black
pepper

225g (8oz) thin asparagus spears,
trimmed and cut into finger-
length pieces

225g (8oz) courgettes, coarsley
grated

115g (4oz) Gruyère cheese, grated

115g (4oz) feta cheese, diced

DRESSING
150ml (5fl oz) olive oil

30ml (2 tbsp) white wine vinegar

5ml (½ tsp) sugar

10ml (2 tsp) Dijon mustard

30ml (2 tbsp) chopped fresh herbs

1 Cook the pasta in plenty of boiling salted water for 10–12 minutes, or until *al dente*. Drain and rinse under cold running water.

2 Cook the asparagus in boiling salted water for 5–7 minutes, or until just tender. Drain and rinse under cold running water.

3 Whisk together all the dressing ingredients and season with salt and pepper to taste.

4 Toss together all the ingredients. Serve immediately, giving it a good stir to mix everything well together before you do so.

TOP TIP
The salad can be made in advance and kept covered in the refrigerator for up to 24 hours.

BEST FAMILY MEALS

CHICKEN SOUP WITH GARLIC AND PARMESAN CROÛTONS

Serves 6
Preparation: 20 minutes
Cooking time: about 1¼ hours
Freezing: suitable at end of stage 2
385 cals per serving

1 small chicken, weighing about 1kg (2lb)

300ml (½ pint) dry white wine

few peppercorns

1–2 red chillis

2 bay leaves

2 rosemary sprigs

1 celery stalk

4 carrots

3 onions

75g (3oz) dried pasta shapes

1 cos lettuce

25g (1oz) butter

1 garlic clove, crushed

30ml (2 tbsp) chopped fresh parsley

salt and freshly ground black pepper

CROÛTONS

50g (2oz) butter, softened

1 garlic clove, crushed

4 thick slices white bread

45ml (3 tbsp) freshly grated Parmesan cheese

1 Put the chicken in a saucepan just large enough to contain it, with the wine, peppercorns, chillis, bay leaves and rosemary. Roughly chop the celery and 3 carrots; quarter 2 onions. Add these to the pan with about 900ml (1½ pints) cold water to almost cover the chicken. Bring to the boil, lower the heat, cover and simmer gently for 1 hour.

2 Leave to cool slightly, then transfer the chicken to a plate and strain the stock. When cool enough to handle, remove the chicken from the bone and tear into bite-sized pieces; set aside.

3 Return the stock to the pan. Bring back to the boil, add the pasta and cook for 5 minutes. Preheat the oven to 200°C/400°F/gas 6.

4 Meanwhile, cut the remaining carrot into fine matchsticks. Peel and chop the remaining onion. Finely shred the lettuce.

5 Melt the butter in a clean pan. Add the onion and garlic and cook for 5 minutes until softened. Add the carrot and cook for 2 minutes. Add the stock and pasta and cook for 5 minutes, then stir in the chicken pieces, lettuce and parsley. Heat gently, stirring, until the lettuce has wilted. Season to taste.

6 Meanwhile, make the croûtons. Mix together the butter and garlic in a small bowl. Remove the crusts from the bread, then spread the garlic butter and sprinkle with Parmesan. Cut into squares and place on a lightly greased baking sheet, spacing them a little apart. Bake in the oven for 8–10 minutes until crisp and golden brown.

7 Serve the chicken soup in warmed bowls, accompanied by the hot garlic and Parmesan croûtons.

TOP TIP
To make the croûtons, cut thick slices from a whole loaf rather than use ready-sliced bread.

MINESTRONE WITH PESTO

Serves 6–8
Preparation: 20 minutes, plus overnight soaking
Cooking time: about 2–2½ hours
Freezing: suitable
540–400 cals per serving

175g (6oz) dried haricot, cannellini or flageolet beans, soaked overnight in cold water

salt and freshly ground black pepper

2.3 litres (4 pints) vegetable stock

1 dried red chilli

450g (1lb) potatoes, peeled and diced

450g (1lb) carrots, peeled and diced

2 large leeks, trimmed and thinly sliced

450g (1lb) courgettes, diced

225g (8oz) French beans, halved

425g (15oz) can chopped tomatoes

125g (4oz) dried pastini (tiny soup pasta)

TO SERVE
pesto sauce (see page 25)

50g (2oz) pecorino or Parmesan cheese, freshly grated

1 Drain the beans and put them in a large saucepan with enough fresh cold water to cover. Bring to the boil and boil steadily for 10 minutes, then lower the heat and simmer for 1–1½ hours or until the beans are tender, adding salt towards the end of the cooking time. Drain thoroughly.

2 Pour the stock into a large pan; add the chilli. Bring to the boil, then add the cooked beans, potatoes, carrots and leeks. Lower the heat, cover and simmer for 25 minutes or until the vegetables are very tender.

3 Add the courgettes, French beans, tomatoes and pasta and season generously with salt and pepper. Simmer, covered, for a further 10 minutes or until the pasta is just cooked.

4 Served as a main course with plenty of good bread. Hand the pesto and grated cheese separately.

TOP TIP
Instead of dried beans, use two 400g (14oz) cans beans. Drain and add to the soup towards the end of stage 3 to heat through.

TAGLIATELLE WITH CHICKEN AND COURGETTES

Serves 4
Preparation: 15 minutes
Cooking time: about 35 minutes
Freezing: not suitable
640 cals per serving

3.6cm (1½ inch) piece fresh root ginger

3 garlic cloves, peeled

3 red chillis

4 boneless chicken breasts, skinned

65g (2½oz) butter

coarse sea salt and freshly ground black pepper

2 small courgettes

45ml (3 tbsp) chopped fresh coriander or tarragon

15ml (1 tbsp) chopped fresh parsley

400g (14oz) tagliatelle

1 Preheat the oven to 190°C/375°F/gas 5. Peel and grate the root ginger. Chop the garlic finely. Halve, deseed and chop the chillis. Arrange the chicken breasts in one layer on a large piece of foil and sprinkle with the ginger, garlic and chillis. Dot with 25g (1oz) of the butter and season with salt and pepper.

2 Wrap the foil tightly to form a parcel and place on a baking sheet. Bake in the oven for 30 minutes or until the chicken is tender and cooked through.

3 Meanwhile, thinly slice the courgettes. Melt the remaining butter in a large frying pan. Add the courgettes and cook over a medium heat, stirring frequently, for 4–5 minutes until tender and just beginning to brown. Stir in the herbs and cook briefly. Remove from the heat.

4 About 5 minutes before the chicken will be ready, cook the pasta in a large pan of boiling salted water according to the packet instructions until it is *al dente*.

5 When the chicken is cooked, carefully lift out, retaining the juices in the foil parcel. Cut the chicken into slices or cubes and return to the foil.

6 Drain the pasta and return to the pan. Add the chicken with its juices and the courgettes, butter and herbs. Toss lightly to mix. Adjust the seasoning to taste and serve at once.

VARIATION
Replace the chicken breasts with 450g (1lb) salmon fillet, skinned. Use only 2 garlic cloves. Cook the salmon in the parcel as above but reduce the cooking time to 20–25 minutes; the fish should be opaque, firm and flake easily.

RIGATONI BAKED WITH SPICY SAUSAGE

Serves 4–6
Preparation: 15–20 minutes
Cooking time: 30–35 minutes
Freezing: not suitable
1000–670 cals per serving

45ml (3 tbsp) extra-virgin olive oil

350g (12oz) uncooked spicy sausage

1 onion

2 garlic cloves

12 black olives

5 sun-dried tomatoes

90ml (3fl oz) dry white wine

30ml (2 tbsp) chopped fresh oregano

15ml (1 tbsp) chopped fresh parsley

2 x 400g (14oz) cans plum tomatoes

salt and freshly ground black pepper

400g (14oz) dried rigatoni

15g (½oz) butter

175g (6oz) mozzarella cheese (preferably smoked), diced

50g (2oz) Parmesan cheese, in one piece

oregano sprigs, to garnish

1 Heat 15ml (1 tbsp) of the oil in a large frying pan, then add the sausage, cut into lengths to fit the pan, if necessary. Fry on a medium-high heat for 4–5 minutes, turning frequently, until lightly browned. Transfer to a plate and cut into slices. Set aside.

2 Peel and chop the onion and garlic. Slice the olives from their stones; dice the sun-dried tomatoes. Add the remaining oil to the frying pan. Stir in the onion and garlic and cook over a medium heat for 5 minutes, until softened but not browned. Return the sliced sausage to the pan and add the wine and herbs. Increase the heat and cook for 3–4 minutes until about two-thirds of the wine has evaporated.

3 Stir in the canned tomatoes and their juice, breaking them up with a wooden spoon. Add the sun-dried tomatoes and olives. Cook, uncovered, over a medium heat for 15–20 minutes until the tomatoes are pulp-like; do not reduce the tomatoes too much. Season to taste.

4 Meanwhile, preheat the oven to 200°C/400°F/gas 6. Cook the rigatoni in a large pan of boiling salted water until almost *al dente* or for about 2 minutes less time than the packet instructions. Drain thoroughly.

5 Butter a baking dish large enough to hold the pasta and sauce. Transfer the pasta to the dish and toss with the sauce. Scatter the mozzarella over the rigatoni. Using a potato peeler, 'shave' the Parmesan cheese over the mozzarella. Bake near the top of the oven for about 15 minutes, until piping hot. Serve at once, garnished with oregano sprigs.

TOP TIP
To reduce the preparation time, use cooked sausages, such as chorizo, instead of raw ones. Omit stage 1, slice the sausages and add at stage 2.

SPAGHETTI WITH LAMB RAGU

Serves 4–6
Preparation: 25 minutes
Cooking time: 2½–3 hours
Freezing: suitable at stage 4
740–495 cals per serving

1 onion

2 garlic cloves

10ml (2 tsp) fennel seeds

2 carrots

2 celery stalks

45ml (3 tbsp) extra-virgin olive oil

350g (12oz) minced lamb

200ml (7fl oz) red wine

45ml (3 tbsp) chopped fresh oregano

1 rosemary sprig

½ cinnamon stick

400g (14oz) can chopped tomatoes

salt and freshly ground black pepper

400g (14oz) dried spaghetti, fettucine or long fusilli

75ml (5 tbsp) freshly grated Parmesan cheese

1 Peel and finely chop the onion and garlic. Lightly crush the fennel seeds. Finely dice the carrots and celery.

2 Heat the oil in a saucepan. Add the onion and garlic and cook over a medium heat for 5 minutes until softened but not browned. Add the fennel seeds and cook for 1 minute, then add the carrot and celery and cook, stirring, for 2 minutes.

3 Add the lamb to the pan and cook for about 7 minutes, breaking up the pieces with a wooden spoon, until browned. Increase the heat and stir in the wine. Let bubble for 4–5 minutes until the liquid has reduced by about half.

4 Add the oregano, rosemary sprig and cinnamon to the pan with the canned tomatoes and their juice. Bring to the boil and season lightly with salt and pepper. Cook, uncovered, on a very low heat for 2½–3 hours, stirring occasionally until the lamb is meltingly tender and the oil separates from the sauce. Remove and discard the cinnamon and rosemary. Spoon off the oil, soaking up any excess with kitchen paper. Adjust the seasoning to taste.

5 Just before serving, cook the spaghetti in a large pan of boiling salted water according to the packet instructions until *al dente*. Drain thoroughly.

6 To serve, toss the ragu with the pasta and about half of the grated Parmesan. Serve at once, sprinkled with the remaining Parmesan.

TOP TIP
The sauce tastes even better if it is prepared ahead, allowed to cool and left to stand for a while. Remove any fat from the surface and reheat thoroughly before serving.

VARIATION
To make a classic Spaghetti alla Bolognese, substitute lean minced beef for the lamb. Replace the rosemary with a few sprigs of fresh thyme.

PASTA WITH TWO-TOMATO SAUCE

Serves 4–6
Preparation: about 12 minutes
Cooking time: 25–30 minutes
Freezing: suitable (sauce only)
570–380 cals per serving

1 onion

2 garlic cloves

50g (2oz) butter

1kg (2lb) ripe tomatoes, preferably plum, or 2 x 400g (14oz) cans plum tomatoes with their juice

45ml (3 tbsp) sun-dried tomato paste (see page 14)

2 oregano sprigs

400g (14oz) dried fusilli, pasta shells or penne

salt and freshly ground black pepper

TO SERVE
20–50g (1–2oz) Parmesan cheese

chopped fresh parsley, to garnish

1 To prepare the sauce, peel and chop the onion and finely chop the garlic. Melt the butter in a saucepan, add the onion and garlic and cook over a medium-low heat for about 8 minutes while preparing the tomatoes.

2 If using fresh tomatoes, first skin them. Immerse in a bowl of boiling water for 30 seconds, then drain and refresh under cold running water. Peel away the skins. Quarter the tomatoes, discard the seeds, then roughly chop the flesh. If using canned plum tomatoes, chop them roughly.

3 Add the tomatoes to the onion and garlic mixture together with the sun-dried tomato paste and oregano sprigs. Cook, uncovered, over a low heat for 25–30 minutes, stirring occasionally, until the sauce is thick and pulpy.

4 Meanwhile, cook the pasta in a large pan of boiling salted water according to the packet instructions until *al dente*. Drain thoroughly in a colander.

5 Discard the oregano and season the sauce with salt and pepper to taste. Add the pasta and toss well to mix. Serve at once, topped with shavings of Parmesan cheese and chopped parsley.

PASTA WITH CHORIZO

Serves 4–6
Preparation: 10 minutes
Cooking time: about 50 minutes
Freezing: suitable
950–630 cals per serving

1 onion

2 garlic cloves

30ml (2 tbsp) olive oil

30ml (2 tbsp) tomato purée

30ml (2 tbsp) mild paprika

1 dried chilli

2 bay leaves

2 fresh thyme sprigs

2 fresh rosemary sprigs

150ml (½ pint) dry red wine

425g (15oz) can chopped
tomatoes

salt and freshly ground black
pepper

450g (1lb) raw chorizo sausage, in
one piece

400–450g (14oz–1lb) fresh or
dried pasta

chopped fresh parsley, to garnish

1 Peel and finely chop the onion. Crush the garlic. Heat the oil in a heavy-based saucepan, add the onion and garlic and sauté for about 5 minutes or until softened. Add the tomato purée and paprika and cook for 2 minutes, stirring all the time.

2 Crumble in the chilli, then add the bay leaves, thyme and rosemary. Pour in the wine and bring to the boil. Cook for 2 minutes, stirring. Add the tomatoes with their juice and bring to the boil again. Lower the heat and simmer gently for 30 minutes. Season generously with salt and pepper.

3 Cut the chorizo sausage into thick slices and add to the sauce. Cook for 15 minutes.

4 Meanwhile, bring a large pan of boiling salted water to the boil. Add the pasta, bring back to the boil and stir once. Cook until *al dente*. Dried pasta will take about 8–12 minutes; fresh pasta 2–3 minutes.

5 Drain the pasta in a colander, shaking it vigorously to remove all water. Divide between warmed individual serving bowls or turn into a large warmed serving bowl. Spoon the sauce on top of the pasta, sprinkle with plenty of chopped parsley and serve immediately.

PASTA WITH PORK, SAGE AND FETA CHEESE

Serves 4
Preparation: 25 minutes
Cooking time: 20 minutes
Freezing: not suitable
890 cals per serving

450g (1lb) pork fillet

125g (4oz) feta cheese

30ml (2 tbsp) chopped fresh sage
or 2.5ml (½ tsp) dried

60ml (4 tbsp) chopped fresh
parsley

salt and freshly ground black
pepper

75g (3oz) butter

1 onion, peeled and sliced

150ml (¼ pint) white wine

150ml (¼ pint) chicken stock

150ml (¼ pint) crème fraîche

350g (12oz) dried papardelle or
tagliatelle

sage sprigs, to garnish

1 Cut the pork into four equal pieces. Bat out between sheets of greaseproof paper until about 3mm (⅛ inch) thick, using a rolling pin or meat mallet.

2 Blend the feta cheese with 15ml (1 tbsp) sage and 30ml (2 tbsp) parsley until smooth. Season with salt and pepper to taste.

3 Divide the cheese mixture between the pieces of pork and spread evenly. Roll up each piece and skewer with a cocktail stick.

4 Melt half of the butter in a heavy-based frying pan (with a lid). Add the onion and fry for 4–5 minutes. Add the pork and fry, turning, for about 2–3 minutes until browned.

5 Pour in the wine and stock. Bring to the boil, then add the remaining herbs and crème fraîche. Cover and simmer for 10–15 minutes or until the pork is tender.

6 Meanwhile, cook the pasta in a large pan of boiling salted water according to the packet instructions until *al dente*. Drain thoroughly and toss with the remaining butter.

7 Remove the pork rolls from the sauce and cut into slices. Divide the pasta between the warmed serving plates, top with the pork and pour over the sauce. Serve at once, garnished with sage.

LEMON TAGLIATELLE WITH SUMMER VEGETABLES AND HERB SAUCE

Serves 4–6
Preparation: 20 minutes, plus pasta
Cooking time: 10 minutes
Freezing: not suitable
715–475 cals per serving

25g (1oz) mixed fresh herbs, such as basil, chervil, chives, dill, parsley, roughly chopped

5ml (1 tsp) dried oregano

120ml (4fl oz) extra-virgin olive oil

700g (1½ lb) mixed summer vegetables to include: asparagus tips, courgettes, French beans, shelled broad beans and/or peas, baby carrots, cherry tomatoes (optional)

2 shallots, peeled and finely chopped

1 garlic clove, peeled and crushed

90ml (6 tbsp) single cream

1 quantity fresh lemon tagliatelle (see pages 12–13), or 400g (14oz) dried tagliatelle

salt and freshly ground black pepper

1 Place the fresh herbs and oregano in a bowl. Add all but 30ml (2 tbsp) of the olive oil. Stir well and set aside for a few hours if possible, to infuse.

2 Prepare the vegetables. Thinly slice the courgettes; trim the asparagus spears; trim the French beans; peel the carrots and halve lengthways if large.

3 Blanch all the vegetables, except the tomatoes, separately, in a large pan of lightly salted boiling water for 1–3 minutes depending on size and the vegetable. Courgette slices need the shortest time followed by asparagus, French beans and broad beans/peas with baby carrots taking the longest.

4 Heat the remaining oil in a large frying pan, add the shallots and garlic and sauté for 5 minutes. Add the vegetables to the pan, stir-fry over a gentle heat and add the herb mixture.

5 Meanwhile, cook the tagliatelle in a large pan of boiling salted water until *al dente*. Fresh pasta will only take 2–3 minutes.

6 Drain the pasta, reserving 60ml (4 tbsp) of the cooking water. Add the pasta and water to the frying pan and toss with the vegetables and herb sauce. Stir in the cream and heat through briefly. Serve at once, seasoned with salt and pepper.

PASTA WITH MEDITERRANEAN VEGETABLES AND WALNUT PASTE

Serves 4–6
Preparation: 25 minutes
Cooking time: 20 minutes
Freezing: not suitable
950–630 cals per serving

1 fennel bulb, sliced

2 small red onions, peeled and cut into wedges

2 courgettes, halved and thinly sliced lengthways

1 large red pepper, cored, seeded and cut into broad strips

6 small tomatoes, halved

45ml (3 tbsp) extra-virgin olive oil

15ml (1 tbsp) chopped fresh thyme

5ml (1 tsp) grated lemon rind

400g (14oz) dried tagliatelle

coarse sea salt and freshly ground black pepper

WALNUT PASTE
150g (5oz) walnuts, roughly chopped

1 garlic clove, peeled and chopped

45ml (3 tbsp) chopped fresh parsley

75ml (5 tbsp) extra-virgin olive oil

50g (2oz) ricotta or other soft cheese

TO GARNISH
thyme sprigs

1 Add the fennel and onions to a large pan of boiling water, bring back to the boil and cook for 2 minutes. Add the courgette strips and cook for a further 1 minute. Drain in a colander and refresh under cold running water. Drain and set aside.

2 Preheat the grill to high. Put the blanched vegetables in a bowl with the red pepper and tomatoes. Add the olive oil, thyme and lemon rind and toss to coat.

3 Transfer the vegetables to the foil-lined grill pan and grill for 15–20 minutes, turning occasionally until they are tender and patched with brown.

4 Meanwhile, cook the tagliatelle in a large pan of boiling salted water according to the packet instructions until *al dente*.

5 While the pasta is cooking, prepare the walnut paste. Put the walnuts and garlic into a food processor and process briefly to chop finely. Add the parsley and process for 1 second. Add the oil and work to a coarse paste. Transfer to a bowl and stir in the ricotta and seasoning.

6 Drain the pasta thoroughly in a colander. Meanwhile, gently heat the walnut paste in the large pasta pan for a few seconds, then remove from the heat, add the pasta and toss to mix. Serve at once, topped with the grilled vegetables, drizzling over any oil and juices from the grill pan.

VARIATION
Try olive paste rather than walnut paste. Either buy ready-made or make your own. To do this, process stoned olives with a chopped garlic clove, olive oil and some freshly chopped herbs.

SPINACH AND RICOTTA RAVIOLI

Serves 4–6
Preparation: 20 minutes, plus resting
Cooking time: 3 minutes
Freezing: suitable at stage 6
765–505 cals per serving

PASTA
400g (14oz) plain white flour

salt

4 medium eggs, beaten

15ml (1 tbsp) olive oil

FILLING
450g (1lb) frozen spinach, thawed and squeezed dry

175g (6oz) fresh ricotta or curd cheese

2.5ml (½ tsp) freshly grated nutmeg

5ml (1 tsp) salt

freshly ground black pepper, to taste

TO FINISH
beaten egg, to seal

75g (3oz) butter, melted

25g (1oz) freshly pared Parmesan cheese

1 To make the pasta, sift the flour and a pinch of salt onto a clean work surface and make a well in the centre with your fist. Pour the beaten eggs and oil into the well. Gradually mix the eggs into the flour, using the fingers of one hand.

2 Knead the pasta until smooth, wrap in cling film and leave it to rest for at least 30 minutes before rolling out. The pasta will be much more elastic after resting.

3 To make the filling, place all the ingredients in a food processor or blender and process until smooth. Cover and refrigerate.

4 Cut the dough in half and re-wrap one piece in cling film. On a lightly floured surface, roll the other piece out thinly into a rectangle. Cover with a clean damp tea towel and repeat with the remaining pasta.

5 Spoon or pipe small rounds, about 5ml (1 tsp), of filling in even rows across one piece of dough, spacing them at 4cm (1½ inch) intervals. Brush the spaces of dough between the mounds with beaten egg to help seal the ravioli. Using a rolling pin, carefully lift the other sheet of pasta over the top. Press down firmly between the pockets of filling, pushing out any trapped air.

6 Cut into squares, using a serrated ravioli cutter or a sharp knife. Transfer to a floured tea towel and leave to rest for 1 hour before cooking.

7 Bring a large saucepan of salted water to the boil. Add the ravioli and cook for about 3 minutes, until puffy. Drain well and toss with the melted butter. Serve topped with slivers of Parmesan.

VARIATION
For a different filling, sauté 125g (4oz) chopped pancetta or thick-cut unsmoked bacon in butter until golden and crisp. Stir in 45ml (3 tbsp) chopped fresh sage, then beat into the ricotta filling. Continue as above.

MACARONI LAYER PIE

Serves 4–6
Preparation: 40–55 minutes
Cooking time: 1¼–1½ hours
Freezing: not suitable
839–559 cals per serving

15ml (1 tbsp) vegetable oil

450g (1lb) minced beef

115g (4oz) onion, peeled and crushed

1 garlic clove, peeled and chopped

400g (14oz) can chopped tomatoes

200ml (7fl oz) chicken or beef stock

5ml (1 tsp) dried mixed herbs

salt and freshly ground black pepper

225g (8oz) dried macaroni

40g (1½oz) butter

45ml (3 tbsp) plain flour

450ml (15fl oz) milk

10ml (2 tsp) Dijon mustard

115g (4oz) Cheddar cheese, grated

1 Heat the oil in a medium saucepan and cook the mince and onion over a high heat for 5–8 minutes, or until they are lightly coloured. Break up the mince as you brown it, spreading it evenly around the pan, to prevent it from forming into lumps.

2 Add the garlic, tomatoes with the juices, stock, herbs and seasoning. Bring to the boil and simmer, uncovered, for about 20 minutes, or until the mince is tender and the liquid well reduced. Adjust the seasoning.

3 Preheat the oven to 200°C/400°F/gas 6. Meanwhile, cook the macaroni in boiling salted water for 10–12 minutes, or until *al dente*. Drain and rinse under cold running water, then drain for 2–3 minutes longer.

4 Layer the mince and pasta alternately in a lightly greased, large deep ovenproof serving dish, ending with a pasta layer on the top.

5 Melt the butter in a saucepan. Add the flour and cook, stirring, for 1–2 minutes before gradually adding the milk. Bring to the boil, then simmer for 2–3 minutes.

6 Off the heat, whisk in the mustard, half the grated Cheddar cheese and seasoning. Pour over the pasta and sprinkle with the remaining grated cheese.

7 Stand the dish on a baking tray and then bake in the oven for 35–40 minutes, or until golden and thoroughly hot. Serve immediately.

SEAFOOD LASAGNE

Serves 6
Preparation: about 35 minutes
Cooking time: 1–1¼ hours
Freezing: not suitable
587 cals per serving

450g (1lb) fresh haddock fillet, skinned

300ml (10fl oz) white wine

slices of carrot, onion and bay leaf for flavouring

salt and freshly ground black pepper

200g (7oz) dried spinach lasagne

150g (5oz) butter

450g (1lb) leeks, trimmed, thickly sliced and washed

1 garlic clove, peeled and crushed

90g (3½oz) plain flour

150ml (5fl oz) single cream

150ml (5fl oz) soured cream

15ml (1 tbsp) chopped fresh dill

225g (8oz) packet seafood cocktail

50g (2oz) Cheddar or Gruyère cheese, grated

30ml (2 tbsp) grated Parmesan cheese

fresh dill and lemon slices, to garnish

1 Preheat the oven to 200°C/400°F/gas 6. Cover the haddock fillet with water and half the wine. Add the flavouring ingredients, season and bring to the boil. Cover and simmer for 5 minutes, or until tender.

2 Lift the fish on to a plate and flake the fish, discarding any bones. Strain the cooking juices and make it up to 1 litre (1¾ pints) with water.

3 Cook the lasagne according to the packet instructions, stirring occasionally with a fork. Drain and immediately run cold water over the pasta. Spread on a clean tea towel and cover.

4 Melt 50g (2oz) of the butter in a medium saucepan and gently cook the leeks and garlic, covered, for about 10 minutes. Remove from the pan using a slotted spoon.

5 Melt the remaining butter. Add the flour and cook, stirring, for 1 minute. Off the heat, stir in the reserved 1 litre (1¾ pints) stock and remaining wine. Bring to the boil, stirring, and cook for 2 minutes. Off the heat, whisk in the cream, soured cream and dill. Season with salt and pepper.

6 Spoon a little of the sauce into a 3 litre (5¼ pint) shallow ovenproof serving dish. Top with a layer of pasta, followed by the haddock, seafood cocktail and leeks, and a little more sauce. Scatter over the grated cheeses.

7 Bake in the oven for 45–50 minutes. Cool slightly before serving, garnished with dill and lemon.

VARIATION
Substitute the seafood cocktail with cooked peeled prawns or any type of cooked fish or shellfish, depending on what is available.

PASTA BAKE

Serves 3–4
Preparation: about 20 minutes
Cooking time: about 40 minutes
Freezing: not suitable
820–615 cals per serving

75g (3oz) Gruyère cheese, grated

good pinch freshly grated nutmeg

salt and freshly ground black
pepper

225g (8oz) dried conchiglie or
farfalle

1 quantity rich tomato sauce (see
page 22)

60ml (3 tbsp) freshly grated
Parmesan cheese

45ml (3 tbsp) dried breadcrumbs

BÉCHAMEL SAUCE
300ml (10fl oz) milk

1 bay leaf

25g (1oz) butter

25g (1oz) plain flour

1 Preheat the oven to 190°C/375°F/gas 5. To make the béchamel sauce, put the milk and bay leaf in a saucepan and slowly bring to the boil. Remove from the heat. Melt the butter in a separate saucepan. Sprinkle in the flour and cook over a low heat for 1–2 minutes, stirring. Remove from the heat.

2 Discard the bay leaf from the milk. Gradually blend the milk into the mixture, stirring well. Bring to the boil slowly and cook, stirring, until the sauce thickens. Simmer very gently for a further 2–3 minutes, then add the cheese and nutmeg, season with salt and pepper and stir until the cheese has melted.

3 Cook the pasta in a large pan of boiling water until *al dente,* or according to the packet instructions. Drain the pasta and mix with the tomato sauce. Spread half this mixture in the bottom of a buttered ovenproof dish and cover with half the béchamel sauce. Repeat the layers, then sprinkle with Parmesan and breadcrumbs.

4 Bake in the oven for 20 minutes, then brown under a hot grill for 5 minutes. Serve immediately.

PASTA WITH TUNA AND OLIVE SAUCE

Serves 4
Preparation: about 20 minutes
Cooking time: 25–30 minutes
Freezing: not suitable
481 cals per serving

50g (2oz) can anchovy fillets

milk, for soaking

15ml (1 tbsp) olive oil

1 onion, peeled and chopped

1 garlic clove, peeled and crushed

5ml (1 tsp) dried marjoram

400g (14oz) can chopped tomatoes

335g (12oz) dried pasta shapes

salt and freshly ground black pepper

200g (7oz) can tuna steaks in brine, well drained and flaked

50g (2oz) black or green olives

30ml (2 tbsp) dry white wine

fresh marjoram, to garnish (optional)

Parmesan cheese, to serve

1 To remove the salt from the anchovies, drain well and place in a bowl. Cover with milk and soak for 20 minutes. Drain, pat dry and chop.

2 To make the sauce, heat the oil in a saucepan and gently cook the onion for 5 minutes. Add the garlic, marjoram and tomatoes with their juices. Bring to the boil and simmer for 15 minutes, stirring occasionally, until slightly thickened.

3 Meanwhile, cook the pasta in boiling salted water for 10–12 minutes, or until *al dente*.

4 Add the tuna fish, anchovies and olives to the sauce. Return to the boil, stirring, then simmer for 2–3 minutes. Stir in the wine and season to taste. Drain the pasta and serve hot with the sauce spooned over. Garnish with fresh marjoram, if wished, and top with shavings of Parmesan.

TOP TIP
There is probably no need to add any salt to the sauce as the anchovies contain enough residual salt to season this dish.

BEST VEGETARIAN DISHES

POTATO GNOCCHI WITH RED PESTO

Serves 4

Preparation: 30 minutes

Cooking time: 20–30 minutes, plus 3 minutes

Freezing: not suitable

980–655 cals per serving

PESTO

1 large red pepper

50g (2oz) fresh basil leaves

1 garlic clove, crushed

30ml (2 tbsp) toasted pine nuts

6 sun-dried tomatoes in oil, drained

2 ripe tomatoes, skinned

45ml (3 tbsp) tomato purée

2.5ml (½ tsp) chilli powder

50g (2oz) freshly grated Parmesan cheese

150ml (¼ pint) olive oil

GNOCCHI

900g (2lb) floury potatoes

salt

50g (2oz) butter

1 egg, beaten

225–275g (8–10oz) plain white flour

basil leaves, to garnish

1 Preheat the grill to high. Place the pepper on the grill rack and grill, turning occasionally, until blackened all over. Place in a covered bowl until cool enough to handle, then peel off the skin. Halve the pepper and remove the core and seeds. Place in a blender or food processor with the remaining pesto ingredients except the oil. Blend until smooth, then with the machine running, slowly add the oil.

2 To make the gnocchi, cook the unpeeled potatoes in boiling water for 20–30 minutes until very tender; drain well. Halve and press the potatoes through a potato ricer, or peel and press through a sieve into a bowl.

3 While still warm, add 5ml (1 tsp) salt, the butter, beaten egg and half of the flour. Lightly mix together, then turn out onto a floured board. Gradually knead in enough of the remaining flour to yield a smooth, soft, slightly sticky dough.

4 Roll the dough into thick sausages, 2.5cm (1 inch) in diameter. Cut into 2cm (³/₄ inch) pieces. Shape the gnocchi by rolling each piece over the back of a fork with your floured thumb, to form ridges on one side and an indentation on the other. Place the gnocchi on a floured tea towel.

5 Bring a large pan of salted water to the boil. Cook the gnocchi in batches. Drop them into the boiling water and cook for 2–3 minutes, until they float to the surface. Remove with a slotted spoon and keep hot while cooking the remainder. Toss with the red pesto and serve immediately, garnished with basil leaves.

HERB GNOCCHI WITH GRILLED TOMATO SAUCE

Serves 4
Preparation: 25 minutes
Cooking time: 25–30 minutes, plus 3 minutes
Freezing: not suitable
245 cals per serving

450g (1lb) floury potatoes

1 egg

5ml (1 tsp) salt

15ml (1 tbsp) finely chopped fresh rosemary

60–75g (2½–3oz) plain flour

SAUCE
450g (1lb) mixed red and yellow cherry tomatoes

2 garlic cloves, peeled and sliced

5ml (1 tsp) grated lemon rind

15ml (1 tbsp) chopped fresh thyme

15ml (1 tbsp) chopped fresh basil

30ml (2 tbsp) olive oil

salt and freshly ground black pepper

pinch of sugar

TO SERVE
extra-virgin olive oil

freshly grated Parmesan cheese

rosemary sprigs, to garnish

1 Preheat the oven to its lowest setting. Cook the potatoes in lightly salted boiling water for 15–20 minutes until cooked; drain well and return to the pan. Set over a gentle heat to dry out the potatoes and leave to cool slightly.

2 Bring a large pan of water to a steady simmer. Mash the potatoes smoothly, then work in the egg, salt, rosemary and enough flour to form a soft dough. Add a little more flour if the mixture is too sticky. Transfer to a piping bag fitted with a large plain nozzle.

3 Meanwhile, make the sauce. Preheat the grill. Halve the tomatoes and place in a flameproof dish. Add the garlic, lemon rind, herbs, oil and seasoning and toss together. Sprinkle over the sugar and grill as close to the heat as possible for 10 minutes until the tomatoes are charred and tender.

4 While the tomatoes are grilling, cook the gnocchi in batches. Pipe about six 5cm (2 inch) lengths directly into the boiling water, using a sharp knife to cut them off at the nozzle. Cook for 3–4 minutes until the gnocchi float to the surface.

5 Remove the gnocchi with a slotted spoon, drain on kitchen paper and transfer to a large warmed bowl. Toss with a little olive oil and keep warm in the oven while cooking the remaining potato mixture.

6 Toss the cooked gnocchi with the grilled tomato sauce. Serve immediately dusted with a little freshly grated Parmesan and garnished with rosemary.

VARIATION
Transfer the cooked gnocchi to 4 individual gratin dishes, spoon over the tomato sauce and top with slices of mozzarella and a little grated Parmesan. Grill for 3–4 minutes and serve at once.

PUMPKIN RAVIOLI WITH BUTTER AND HERBS

Serves 4
Preparation: about 45 minutes
Cooking time: 1¼ hours
Freezing: suitable at end of stage 5
490 cals per serving

PASTA DOUGH
1 quantity basic pasta dough (see pages 12–13)

FILLING
450g (1lb) wedge pumpkin

50g (2oz) walnuts, finely chopped

30ml (2 tbsp) olive oil

50g (2oz) provolone or Parmesan cheese, finely grated

20ml (1½ tbsp) chopped fresh basil

20ml (1½ tbsp) chopped fresh parsley

1 egg yolk

freshly grated nutmeg, to taste

30ml (2 tbsp) double cream

salt and freshly ground black pepper

TO SERVE
25g (1oz) butter, melted

chopped fresh herbs, to taste

1 For the filling, preheat the oven to 190°C/375°F/gas 5. Brush the pumpkin flesh with the oil and bake in the oven for about 1 hour until soft. Meanwhile, make the pasta dough, wrap it in cling film and leave it to rest for 20 minutes.

2 Allow the cooked pumpkin to cool slightly, then scrape the flesh into a large bowl and mash until smooth. Add all the other filling ingredients and mix well.

3 If rolling out the pasta by hand, divide in half and roll into 2 sheets. If using a pasta machine, roll manageable portions into strips (see pages 14–16). Either way, roll out as thinly as possible. Keep covered with cling film to prevent the sheets drying out.

4 Take a strip of pasta 10–12cm (4–5 inches) wide. Spoon on heaped teaspoonfuls of stuffing at 6cm (2½ inch) intervals. Brush the edges and between the stuffing with a little water to seal. Cut between the stuffing at 6cm (2½ inch) intervals and cut neatly along the long edges. Repeat to use all of the pasta and stuffing, to make 20–24 ravioli.

5 Bring a large saucepan of salted water to the boil. Cook the ravioli in batches for about 3 minutes until the sealed edges are *al dente*. Drain thoroughly and transfer to a warmed serving dish. Add the butter, herbs, salt and pepper. Toss lightly to coat and serve at once.

VARIATION
For a version that meat-eaters will love, replace the walnuts with 75g (3oz) prosciutto or Parma ham, finely chopped.

TAGLIATELLE WITH PUMPKIN AND BLUE CHEESE SAUCE

Serves 4–6
Preparation: 15 minutes
Cooking time: about 12 minutes
Freezing: not suitable
930–620 cals per serving

350g (12oz) wedge pumpkin

1 garlic clove

25g (1oz) butter

30ml (2 tbsp) chopped fresh parsley

300ml (½ pint) extra-thick double cream

1.25ml (¼ tsp) freshly grated nutmeg

400g (14oz) dried tagliatelle, pappardelle or fusilli

175g (6oz) dolcelatte cheese

salt and freshly ground black pepper

TO GARNISH
30ml (2 tbsp) toasted pine nuts

15ml (1 tbsp) chopped fresh parsley

1 Discard the seeds and remove the skin from the pumpkin. Grate the flesh, using a food processor or by hand. Crush the garlic clove.

2 Melt the butter in a large frying pan. Add the grated pumpkin and garlic and cook over a medium heat, stirring, for about 5 minutes, until softened. Stir in the parsley, cream and nutmeg, and continue cooking for 2 minutes.

3 Cook the pasta in a large pan of boiling salted water until *al dente* or according to the packet instructions.

4 Cut the dolcelatte into small pieces and add to the sauce. Heat gently, stirring until melted. Season with salt and pepper to taste.

5 To serve, drain the pasta thoroughly in a colander and return to the pan. Add the sauce and toss well to mix. Transfer to a warmed serving bowl or plates and serve at once, sprinkled with toasted pine nuts and chopped parsley.

TOP TIP
The easiest way to grate pumpkin is to use a food processor fitted with a medium grating disc.

VARIATION
Replace the dolcelatte with 175g (6oz) garlic and herb-flavoured cheese.

CAPELLINI WITH LEEKS, PEAS AND SAFFRON

Serves 4–6
Preparation: 10 minutes
Cooking time: 15 minutes
Freezing: not suitable
925–615 cals per serving

1.25ml (¼ tsp) saffron threads, crumbled

350g (12oz) leeks

50g (2oz) butter

150g (5oz) frozen peas, thawed

400g (14oz) dried capellini, paglia e fieno or spaghetti

300ml (½ pint) extra-thick double cream

90ml (6 tbsp) freshly grated Parmesan cheese

salt and freshly ground black pepper

chervil or parsley sprigs, to garnish

1 Put the saffron in a small bowl, cover with 60ml (4 tbsp) boiling water and leave to stand. Thinly slice the leeks. Melt the butter in a large frying pan. Add the leeks and cook over a medium heat, stirring, for 7–8 minutes to soften. Add the peas and continue cooking for a further 3 minutes.

2 Meanwhile, cook the pasta in a large pan of boiling salted water until *al dente*, or according to the packet instructions.

3 Add the saffron liquid and the cream to the leeks and peas. Heat gently until simmering. Stir in half of the Parmesan cheese and remove from the heat. Season with salt and pepper.

4 Drain the pasta thoroughly and return to the pan. Add the sauce and toss lightly to mix. Add the remaining Parmesan cheese and toss again. Serve at once, garnished with chervil or parsley.

VARIATION
For non-vegetarians, add 225g (8oz) cooked peeled prawns to the sauce once the pasta is cooked. Reheat gently as above.

FRIED COURGETTE RIBBONS WITH LINGUINI

Serves 4–6
Preparation: about 30 minutes
Cooking time: 20 minutes
Freezing: not suitable
850–565 cals per serving

SAUCE
1 onion

1 garlic clove

45ml (3 tbsp) olive oil

400g (14oz) can chopped tomatoes

45ml (3 tbsp) chopped fresh basil or oregano

salt and freshly ground black pepper

45ml (3 tbsp) double cream

COURGETTE RIBBONS
350g (12oz) small courgettes

2 eggs

225g (8oz) dry white breadcrumbs

25g (1oz) freshly grated Parmesan cheese

10ml (2 tsp) dried thyme

oil, for deep-frying

TO FINISH
400g (14oz) dried linguini

45ml (3 tbsp) freshly grated Parmesan cheese

balsamic vinegar, to serve

1 First, prepare the sauce. Peel and chop the onion and garlic. Heat the oil in a saucepan, add the onion and garlic and cook over a medium heat, stirring frequently, for 5 minutes, to soften. Add the tomatoes and herbs and bring to the boil. Lower the heat and simmer for 10 minutes. Season with salt and pepper. Purée the sauce in a blender or food processor, then sieve the mixture back into the pan. Stir in the cream; set aside.

2 Using a vegetable peeler and pressing firmly, pare the courgettes into long, fairly thin ribbons. Lightly beat the eggs in a shallow bowl. In a separate shallow bowl, mix the breadcrumbs with the Parmesan, thyme, salt and pepper.

3 Heat the oil for deep frying. Dip the courgette ribbons, one at a time, first into the beaten egg and then into the breadcrumb mixture to coat.

4 Cook the pasta in a large pan of boiling salted water until *al dente* or according to the packet instructions.

5 Meanwhile, fry the courgette ribbons, in batches, in the hot oil for 1–2 minutes, until golden and crisp. Drain on kitchen paper then transfer to a plate and keep hot.

6 Gently reheat the tomato sauce. Drain the pasta thoroughly, then return to the pan. Add the sauce and Parmesan and toss lightly. Transfer to a warmed shallow serving dish or individual plates. Pile the courgette ribbons on top and serve at once, accompanied by balsamic vinegar, for sprinkling.

TOP TIP
The courgette ribbons take a little time to prepare, so to compensate the simple sauce can be prepared ahead.

PASTA WITH CAPER SAUCE AND GRILLED CHEESE

Serves 4–6
Preparation: about 30 minutes
Cooking time: 15 minutes
Freezing: not suitable
755–505 cals per serving

2 red peppers

2 onions

2 garlic cloves

90ml (6 tbsp) extra-virgin olive oil

45ml (3 tbsp) chopped fresh parsley

50g (2oz) capers in wine vinegar, drained (drained weight)

salt and freshly ground black pepper

400g (14oz) dried penne, rigatoni or tagliatelle

225g (8oz) halloumi cheese

1 Preheat the grill to hot. Grill the whole peppers, turning occasionally until the skin is blistered and blackened all over. This will take about 20 minutes. Cool slightly then, over a bowl to catch the juices, peel away the charred skin and remove the seeds. Cut the flesh into strips and add to the bowl; set aside.

2 Meanwhile, peel and chop the onions and garlic. Heat 75ml (5 tbsp) olive oil in a large frying pan. Add the onions and cook over a medium heat, stirring frequently, for 7–8 minutes until soft. Stir in the garlic and continue cooking for 2–3 minutes until the onion is golden. Stir in the parsley and transfer the mixture to a food processor.

3 Rinse the capers thoroughly to remove any vinegar and add to the food processor. Season with salt and pepper, then process the mixture very briefly to coarsely chop.

4 Cook the pasta in a large pan of boiling salted water until *al dente* or according to the packet instructions.

5 Meanwhile, cut the halloumi into 1cm (½ inch) cubes. Place these in a baking tin large enough to take them in one layer. Add the remaining 15ml (1 tbsp) olive oil and plenty of pepper. Toss to coat the cheese cubes and grill, stirring occasionally, for about 8 minutes until evenly golden on all sides.

6 Drain the pasta thoroughly and return to the large saucepan. Add the caper sauce and reserved pepper strips. Toss to mix. Transfer to a warmed serving bowl or individual plates and sprinkle with the grilled cheese cubes. Serve at once.

> TOP TIP
> If you can't find halloumi, use a firm goat's cheese log, cut into slices.

SPAGHETTINI WITH WILD MUSHROOMS AND SAGE

Serves 4–6
Preparation: 25 minutes, plus soaking time
Cooking time: 20 minutes
Freezing: not suitable
660–440 cals per serving

15g (½oz) dried porcini mushrooms

575g (1lb) mixed fresh mushrooms (field, chestnut, oyster, chanterelles or other wild types, if available)

3 shallots

2–3 garlic cloves

75ml (5 tbsp) extra-virgin olive oil

300ml (½ pint) dry white wine

30ml (2 tbsp) chopped fresh sage

30ml (2 tbsp) chopped fresh parsley

salt and freshly ground black pepper

400g (14oz) dried spaghettini

25–40g (1–1½oz) Parmesan cheese, to serve

1 To reconstitute the dried mushrooms, put them in a small bowl and pour on 125ml (4fl oz) boiling water. Leave to soak for 20 minutes then drain, reserving the soaking liquor. Rinse and chop the mushrooms.

2 To prepare the fresh mushrooms, wipe them clean and trim off any roots. Slice the large field mushrooms; quarter the chestnut mushrooms; leave the oyster mushrooms and any others whole (unless they are very large). Peel and chop the shallots and garlic.

3 Heat the olive oil in a large frying pan. Add the shallots and sauté over a medium heat for 5 minutes until softened. Stir in the garlic and cook for a further 1–2 minutes.

4 Add the chopped dried mushrooms to the frying pan with the soaking liquor and the wine. Bring to the boil, then lower the heat a little and allow to bubble for 8–10 minutes until the liquid has reduced by about half.

5 Add all the fresh mushrooms, except the oyster mushrooms, to the pan with the sage. Cook for about 6 minutes until they are tender. Stir in the oyster mushrooms, parsley and seasoning. Cook for a further 2 minutes.

6 Meanwhile, cook the spaghettini in a large pan of boiling salted water until *al dente* or according to the packet instructions. Drain thoroughly and return to the pan.

7 Add the mushroom mixture to the pasta and toss lightly to mix. Adjust the seasoning and serve at once, sprinkled with shavings of Parmesan.

TOP TIP
To clean fresh mushrooms, wipe them with a damp piece of absorbent kitchen paper or cloth.

PASTA WITH ROASTED VEGETABLES

Serves 4

Preparation: 20 minutes

Cooking time: 20–25 minutes

Freezing: not suitable

485 cals per serving

1 fennel bulb

2 yellow peppers

1 red onion

2 garlic cloves, peeled

15ml (1 tbsp) olive oil

150ml (¼ pint) low-fat bio yogurt

125g (4oz) ricotta or other curd cheese

30ml (2 tbsp) chopped fresh basil

30ml (2 tbsp) chopped fresh parsley

salt and freshly ground black pepper

350g (12oz) fresh pappardelle or tagliatelle

30ml (2 tbsp) freshly grated Parmesan cheese

30ml (2 tbsp) black olives

30ml (2 tbsp) capers

flat-leafed parsley, to garnish

1 Preheat the oven to 220°C/425°F/gas 7. Trim the fennel and cut lengthways into slices, about 2.5cm (1 inch) thick; reserve a few fronds for garnish. Cut the peppers in half, remove the seeds and core and cut into broad 2.5cm (1 inch) long strips. Peel and slice the onion. Place the vegetables, including the whole garlic cloves, on a baking sheet. Brush lightly with the oil and bake in the oven for 20–25 minutes, until browning along the edges.

2 Meanwhile, place the yogurt, cheese and milk in a bowl. Add the basil and parsley, season liberally with black pepper and mix to form a pale green sauce. Transfer the sauce to a pan and heat through gently.

3 Cook the pasta in a large pan of boiling salted water for 2–3 minutes, until *al dente*; drain thoroughly. Add to the sauce with the Parmesan and toss well. Transfer to a warmed serving dish.

4 Remove the vegetables from the oven, mix in the olives and capers and serve on top of the pasta. Garnish with flat-leafed parsley and the reserved fennel fronds. Serve at once.

> *VARIATION*
>
> *For a roasted ratatouille sauce, replace the fennel with 1 small aubergine, a few tomatoes and 1–2 courgettes (omit the capers). Then roast as above.*

SPINACH TAGLIATELLE WITH BLUE CHEESE

Serves 4
Preparation: 5 minutes
Cooking time: 2–12 minutes
Freezing: not suitable
695 cals per serving

4–6 spring onions

400g (14oz) fresh or dried spinach tagliatelle

150g (5oz) ricotta cheese

150g (5oz) blue Stilton cheese

150g (5oz) crème fraîche

15ml (1 tbsp) chopped fresh coriander leaves

coarse sea salt and freshly ground black pepper

1 Trim the spring onions and finely chop them. Cook the tagliatelle in a large pan of boiling salted water until *al dente*. Fresh pasta will take 2–3 minutes to cook, otherwise refer to the packet instructions.

2 While the pasta is cooking, crumble the ricotta and Stilton cheeses together into a bowl. Add the crème fraîche and stir well to mix.

3 Drain the pasta thoroughly in a colander and turn into a heated serving dish. Immediately add the crumbled cheese mixture, spring onions and chopped coriander leaves. Using two forks, lift the tagliatelle to coat with the sauce. Garnish with sprigs of coriander and serve immediately.

THREE CHEESE SPAGHETTINI WITH CELERY

Serves 4
Preparation: 20 minutes
Cooking time: 15 minutes
Freezing: not suitable
690 cals per serving

150g (5oz) spaghettini

salt and freshly ground black pepper

50g (2oz) pine nuts

25g (1oz) butter

5 celery sticks, thinly sliced

150ml (¼ pint) single cream

75g (3oz) mascarpone cheese

15ml (1 tbsp) wholegrain mustard (optional)

30ml (2 tbsp) white wine vinegar

45ml (3 tbsp) extra-virgin olive oil

125g (4oz) blue cheese, such as Roquefort or Blue d'Auvergne, crumbled

100g (3 oz) goat's cheese log, sliced into 4 rounds

rocket or watercress leaves, to serve

1 Cook the pasta in a large pan of boiling salted water until *al dente*. Meanwhile, toast the pine nuts in a frying pan until golden, then remove and set aside. Melt the butter in the pan, add the celery and fry gently for about 8 minutes until softened.

2 In the meantime, beat the cream with the mascarpone cheese, mustard, if using, seasoning and 15ml (1 tbsp) wine vinegar until smooth.

3 Drain the pasta and toss with the olive oil, the remaining wine vinegar and more seasoning. Add the celery and pine nuts and toss to mix.

4 Preheat the grill to high. Season the slices of goat's cheese and grill for 3–4 minutes until golden. Turn the pasta mixture onto warmed serving plates and spoon over the cream sauce. Scatter the blue cheese and slices of goat's cheese. Serve topped with plenty of rocket or watercress leaves, accompanied by a warm nutty bread, such as walnut or mixed grain.

BEETROOT RAVIOLI WITH SPINACH RICOTTA FILLING

Serves 4 (or 6 as a starter)
Preparation: 40 minutes, plus pasta
Cooking time: 10 minutes
Freezing: suitable (see Top Tip)
765–605 cals per serving

175g (6oz) frozen leaf spinach, thawed

15ml (1 tbsp) extra-virgin olive oil

1 small onion, peeled and chopped

1 garlic clove, peeled and crushed

finely grated rind of 1 lemon

175g (6oz) ricotta cheese

40g (1½oz) Parmesan cheese, freshly grated

1 egg yolk

salt and freshly ground black pepper

1 quantity fresh beetroot pasta dough (see page 13)

120ml (4fl oz) hazelnut oil

25g (1oz) hazelnuts, finely chopped

15–30ml (1–2 tbsp) chopped fresh tarragon

tarragon sprigs, to garnish

Parmesan shavings, to serve

1 Squeeze the spinach to remove all excess liquid, then place in a blender or food processor.

2 Heat the olive oil in a small frying pan, add the onion, garlic and lemon rind and fry for 5 minutes until softened. Remove from the heat and let cool slightly.

3 Add the onion mixture to the spinach and blend until fairly smooth. Add the ricotta, Parmesan, egg yolk and seasoning. Work briefly until evenly blended, then transfer to a bowl. Cover and chill for 30 minutes.

4 To shape the ravioli, roll out the pasta dough, using a pasta machine if possible, to form 8 pasta sheets (see pages 14–16). Lay one sheet on a well-floured surface and place 5 heaped teaspoons of the spinach filling on the pasta at 5cm (2 inch) intervals.

5 Using a wet pastry brush, dampen around the mounds of filling. Lay the second sheet of pasta on top and press around the mounds to seal well. Cut into squares with a knife or pasta wheel and place on a floured tea towel. Repeat with the other pasta sheets to make 20 ravioli in total.

6 Bring a large pan of water to a rolling boil with 10ml (2 tbsp) sea salt added. Meanwhile, heat the hazelnut oil in a deep-frying pan. Add the nuts and fry for about 1 minute until turning golden. Remove from the heat. Plunge the ravioli into the fast boiling water, return to the boil and cook for 3 minutes or until *al dente*.

7 Drain the pasta, reserving 60ml (4 tbsp) cooking water and toss with the oil, nuts and tarragon. Add the reserved water, season with salt and pepper to taste and stir briefly. Serve at once, garnished with tarragon and topped with shavings of fresh Parmesan.

TOP TIP
These ravioli may be frozen. After cooking, refresh under cold water and pat dry. Toss with 30ml (2 tbsp) olive oil and transfer to a large freezer bag. Seal and freeze for up to 1 month. Thaw at room temperature and cook in boiling water for 2 minutes before adding to the sauce.

SPAGHETTINI AND ALMOND 'RÖSTI'

Serves 4
Preparation: 20 minutes
Cooking time: 30 minutes
Freezing: not suitable
475 cals per serving

50g (2oz) flaked almonds

90ml (6 tbsp) oil

2 medium onions, thinly sliced

1 garlic clove, crushed

150g (5oz) spaghettini or
paglia e fieno

salt and freshly ground black
pepper

60ml (4 tbsp) chopped fresh
coriander

10ml (2 tsp) cumin seeds, crushed

40g (1½oz) ground almonds

MANGO RELISH
1 large, ripe mango, peeled,
stoned and finely chopped

5g (¼oz) preserved stem ginger,
finely chopped, plus 15ml (1 tbsp
syrup from the jar)

¼ red pepper, seeded and diced

10–15ml (2–3 tsp) white wine
vinegar

TO GARNISH
lemon wedges

chopped coriander

1 First make the relish. Lightly mash the chopped mango flesh in a bowl to give a more pulpy texture. Add the chopped ginger with the syrup, red pepper, seasoning and vinegar to taste. Mix well, then transfer to a serving dish; cover and chill.

2 Toast the almonds in a medium, non-stick frying pan, then remove from the pan and set aside. Heat 30ml (2 tbsp) oil in the pan, add the onions and garlic, and fry gently for about 12 minutes until very soft.

3 Meanwhile, add the pasta to a large pan of boiling salted water and cook until *al dente*. Drain the pasta and toss with the onions, toasted almonds, coriander, cumin, ground almonds and seasoning until thoroughly combined.

4 Heat 30ml (2 tbsp) oil in the frying pan. Turn the pasta mixture into the pan and spread to an even layer, scattering any ingredients left in the bowl over the surface. Pack the mixture down lightly and cook gently for about 12 minutes until the underside is golden.

5 Carefully invert the cake onto a baking sheet. Heat the remaining 30ml (2 tbsp) of the oil in the pan. Slide the pasta back into the pan and fry gently for another 5 minutes.

6 Cut the 'rösti' into wedges. Serve with the mango relish, lemon wedges and a scattering of coriander.

TOP TIP
You can prepare the relish and 'rösti' mixture ahead to the end of stage 4, ready for last-minute cooking.

VARIATION
Divide the 'rösti' mixture into 4 portions and shape into individual cakes. Cook as above, pressing well down. Serve garnished with coriander sprigs.

PASTA WITH GRILLED ASPARAGUS AND BROAD BEANS

Serves 4
Preparation: 20 minutes
Cooking time: 12–15 minutes
Freezing: not suitable
665 cals per serving

225g (8oz) shelled broad beans

salt and freshly ground black pepper

350g (12oz) dried penne or other pasta shapes

450g (1lb) asparagus, trimmed and halved across

SAUCE
190ml (6 tbsp) extra-virgin olive oil

2 garlic cloves, peeled and crushed

grated rind and juice of 1 lemon

45ml (3 tbsp) chopped fresh mint

60ml (4 tbsp) single cream

60ml (4 tbsp) grated pecorino or Parmesan cheese

1 Blanch the broad beans in a large saucepan of lightly salted water for 2 minutes, then drain, reserving the water. Refresh the beans under cold running water and remove the tough outer skins.

2 Bring the reserved water to a rolling boil, add the pasta, return to the boil and cook until *al dente*, or according to the packet instructions.

3 Meanwhile, preheat the grill. Place the asparagus on the grill rack, brush with a little oil and grill for 3–4 minutes on each side until charred and tender.

4 While the pasta is cooking, heat 30ml (2 tbsp) oil in a pan, add the garlic and lemon rind and fry gently for 3 minutes until golden. Add the beans, mint and cream and heat gently.

5 Drain the cooked pasta and immediately toss with the remaining oil. Add the asparagus and bean sauce, cheese and lemon juice. Toss to mix and season with salt and pepper to taste. Serve immediately.

VARIATION
When in season, try using fresh peas in place of the broad beans.

LASAGNETTE WITH COURGETTES AND SUN-DRIED TOMATOES

Serves 4
Preparation: 25 minutes
Cooking time: about 10 minutes
Freezing: not suitable
625 cals per serving

250g (9oz) dried lasagnette

8 small, thin courgettes

salt and freshly ground black pepper

15ml (1 tbsp) olive oil

8 sun-dried tomatoes in oil, cut into wide strips

finely pared rind of 1 lemon, shredded

6 large basil leaves

SAUCE
1 tomato, quartered

50g (2oz) sun-dried tomatoes in oil, drained and roughly chopped

2 garlic cloves, peeled and chopped

50g (2oz) pine nuts

50g (2oz) Parmesan cheese, freshly grated

30ml (2 tbsp) olive oil

30ml (2 tbsp) oil from the sun-dried tomato jar

juice of 1 lemon

10ml (2 tsp) grated horseradish (optional)

5–10ml (1–2 tsp) soft brown sugar, to taste

TO GARNISH
basil sprigs

1 Break the lasagnette strips in half. Pare the courgettes into long thin ribbons, using a swivel vegetable peeler or mandolin.

2 To make the sauce, put the fresh tomato, sun-dried tomatoes and garlic in a blender or food processor and work to a purée. Add the remaining ingredients together with 30ml (2 tbsp) warm water and work until evenly blended. Season to taste and add a little more sugar if required. If the sauce is too thick, thin with a little more water. Transfer to a serving bowl.

3 Cook the lasagnette in a large saucepan of boiling salted water according to the packet instructions until *al dente*.

4 Meanwhile, heat the oil in a frying pan and quickly stir-fry the courgette ribbons, in batches, for 2–3 minutes or until just *al dente*. Remove from the heat and add the sun-dried tomatoes and lemon rind.

5 Drain the pasta well and toss with the courgette mixture and shredded basil. Transfer to a warmed serving bowl and garnish with the basil leaves. Serve the sauce separately at room temperature.

TORTELLONI WITH ROASTED SQUASH AND SAGE BUTTER

Serves 4 (or 6 as a starter)
Preparation: 40 minutes, plus pasta and chilling
Cooking time: 23 minutes
Freezing: tortelloni suitable at end of stage 5 (thaw before cooking)
655–640 cals per serving

300g (10oz) butternut squash, peeled and seeded – ie 225g (8oz) flesh – cubed

1 garlic clove, peeled and crushed

10ml (2 tsp) chopped fresh thyme

30ml (2 tbsp) olive oil

75g (3oz) ricotta cheese

25g (1oz) Parmesan cheese, freshly grated

pinch of freshly grated nutmeg

squeeze of lemon juice

salt and freshly ground black pepper

1 quantity basic pasta dough (see pages 12–13)

125g (4oz) unsalted butter, softened

30ml (2 tbsp) chopped fresh sage leaves

freshly grated Parmesan cheese, to serve (optional)

1 Preheat the oven to 225°C/425°F/gas 7. Place the cubed squash in a small roasting pan with the garlic, thyme and oil. Toss well and roast in the oven for 20 minutes until softened. Mash with a potato masher and set aside to cool.

2 Transfer the cooled squash purée to a bowl and beat in the ricotta, Parmesan, nutmeg, lemon juice and seasoning. Cover and chill for 30 minutes.

3 Divide the dough into 8 pieces and roll out each one, using a pasta machine if possible, to a thin sheet (see pages 14–16). Keep all except one of the pasta sheets covered with cling film. Using a plain 6cm (2 inch) pastry cutter, stamp out 6 rounds from the single pasta sheet. If rolling the pasta dough by hand, divide into 4 pieces and roll out on a floured surface as thinly as possible. Stamp out 12 rounds from each sheet.

4 Place 5ml (1 tsp) of the squash mixture in the middle of each round. Brush the edge of one half of each round with water, then fold the other half over to enclose the filling. Press the edges together to seal well.

5 Curve the semi-circular parcel around your finger and pinch the ends together, turning the sealed edge up to form a neat curved tortelloni as you do so. Place on a well-floured tea towel. Repeat with the remaining pasta and filling to make 48 tortelloni.

6 Cook the tortelloni in a large pan of boiling salted water for 2–3 minutes until *al dente*. Drain well.

7 At the same time, melt the butter with the sage in a large frying pan until foaming. Add the tortelloni and toss well. Serve at once with black pepper, and Parmesan, if wished.

VEGETARIAN BOLOGNESE SAUCE

Serves 8
Preparation: 5–10 minutes
Cooking time: about 45 minutes
Freezing: not suitable
252 cals per serving

30ml (2 tbsp) olive oil

1 celery stick, washed and finely chopped

2 carrots, peeled and finely chopped

1 onion, peeled and finely chopped

115g (4oz) mushrooms, wiped and finely chopped

2 garlic cloves, peeled and crushed

45ml (3 tbsp) tomato purée

2 x 400g (14oz) cans chopped tomatoes

300ml (10fl oz) dry red wine

600ml (20fl oz) vegetable stock

1 bay leaf

1 bouquet garni

5ml (1 tsp) yeast extract savoury spread

5ml (1 tsp) sugar

salt and freshly ground black pepper

freshly grated nutmeg

1 cinnamon stick

175g (6oz) soya mince, dried weight

freshly cooked pasta, to serve

1 Heat the oil in a large, heavy-based saucepan and fry the celery, carrots, onion, mushrooms and garlic for about 5 minutes, or until softened.

2 Add the tomato purée and fry for 1 minute, then add all the remaining ingredients, except the parsley.

3 Bring to the boil, then reduce the heat, cover and simmer gently for 30–40 minutes, or until the soya mince is very tender.

4 Stir in the parsley and season with more salt, pepper and nutmeg, if necessary. Remove the cinnamon stick, bay leaf and bouquet garni and serve with freshly cooked pasta.

VARIATION
To make a spicy version, add 1–2 fresh chopped green chillies instead of the bay leaf and bouquet garni.

SPAGHETTI WITH RATATOUILLE SAUCE

Serves 4
Preparation: about 25 minutes
Cooking time: about 40 minutes
Freezing: not suitable
437 cals per serving

1 aubergine, diced

salt and freshly ground black pepper

1 onion, peeled and finely chopped

1 garlic clove, peeled and crushed

1 red pepper, seeded and cut into thin strips

3 medium courgettes, thinly sliced

335g (12oz) tomatoes, skinned and finely sliced

10ml (2 tsp) chopped fresh basil

400g (14oz) dried wholewheat pasta

fresh basil, to garnish

1 Spread out the aubergine on a plate and sprinkle with salt. Leave for 20 minutes to remove the bitter flavour.

2 Tip the aubergine into a sieve and rinse under cold running water. Put into a large, heavy-based pan with the onion, garlic, pepper, courgettes, tomatoes and basil. Season to taste with salt and pepper.

3 Cover and cook over moderate heat for 30 minutes, shaking the pan and stirring the vegetables frequently to encourage the juices to flow.

4 Meanwhile, cook the spaghetti in boiling salted water for 8–12 minutes, or until *al dente*. Drain well.

5 Place the spaghetti in a warmed serving dish. Taste and adjust the seasoning of the ratatouille sauce, then pour it over the spaghetti. Garnish with basil and serve immediately. Hand the Parmesan cheese separately.

PASTA WITH LEEKS AND FROMAGE FRAIS

Serves 2

Preparation: about 5 minutes

Cooking time: about 35 minutes

Freezing: not suitable

1012 cals per serving

45ml (3 tbsp) olive oil

225g (8oz) leeks, trimmed, sliced and washed

150ml (5fl oz) vegetable stock

225g–275g (8–10oz) dried pasta

salt and freshly ground black pepper

300ml (10fl oz) fromage frais

15ml (1 tbsp) horseradish relish

chopped fresh parsley, to garnish

1 Heat the oil in a saucepan and cook the leeks over a low heat for 4–5 minutes, or until the leeks begin to soften. Add the stock and bring to the boil. Simmer, covered, for 15–20 minutes, or until the leeks are very soft.

2 Meanwhile, cook the pasta in boiling salted water for 8–12 minutes, or until *al dente*.

3 Stir the fromage frais and horseradish into the leek mixture. Season with salt and pepper and heat gently, without boiling, stirring all the time.

4 Drain the pasta and transfer to a warmed serving bowl. Pour the sauce over the pasta and serve, sprinkled with parsley.

MUSHROOM LASAGNE

Serves 6
Preparation: about 25 minutes
Cooking time: 1–1¼ hours
Freezing: not suitable
655 cals per serving

225g (8oz) frozen leaf spinach, thawed

225g (8oz) dried lasagne

salt and freshly ground black pepper

115g (4oz) butter or margarine

900g (2lb) mixed mushrooms, such as button, flat and brown cap (chestnut), wiped and quartered or sliced

30ml (2 tbsp) lemon juice

75g (3oz) plain flour

600ml (20fl oz) milk

600ml (20fl oz) vegetable stock

freshly grated nutmeg, to taste

2 garlic cloves, peeled and crushed

175g (6oz) Gruyère cheese, grated

50g (2oz) fresh white breadcrumbs

1 Preheat the oven to 200°C/400°F/gas 6. Drain the spinach and squeeze out any excess liquid. Chop finely.

2 Cook the pasta in a large saucepan of boiling water until *al dente*, or according to the packet instructions. Drain and rinse under cold running water. Spread the pasta out on a clean tea towel and cover with a damp tea towel until required.

3 Melt half the butter in a large pan. Add the mushrooms and lemon juice, and season with salt and pepper to taste. Cover and cook over a fairly high heat for 4–6 minutes, or until the mushrooms are tender. Remove from the pan with a slotted spoon, then bubble the juices to evaporate any excess moisture until there is only fat left in the saucepan.

4 Melt the remaining butter in the same saucepan. Carefully stir in the flour and cook for 1–2 minutes before slowly blending in the milk and stock. Gradually bring to the boil, making sure that you keep stirring all the time, and cook for 1–2 minutes or until boiling and thickened. Mix in the nutmeg, garlic and spinach. Taste and adjust the seasoning if necessary.

5 Spoon a little of the sauce into the base of a 3 litre (5 pint) ovenproof dish. Top with a layer of mushrooms. Spoon over more of the sauce, then continue layering the ingredients, finishing with the sauce. Sprinkle the Gruyère and breadcrumbs on top.

6 Stand the dish on a baking tray and bake in the oven for 45–60 minutes. Serve immediately.

BEST SPECIAL OCCASION DISHES

PASTA WITH CHICKEN AND NIÇOISE SAUCE

Serves 4
Preparation: 10 minutes
Cooking time: about 20 minutes
Freezing: suitable (sauce only)
640 cals per serving

2 shallots or 1 onion

2 garlic cloves

1 hot red chilli

2 chicken breast fillets, skinned

45ml (3 tbsp) virgin olive oil

2 fresh thyme sprigs

400g (14oz) can chopped tomatoes

generous splash red wine

2 small courgettes (optional)

about 450–700g (1–1½lb) dried pasta ribbons, such as papardelle or tagliatelle

handful of black and green olives

15ml (1 tbsp) capers (optional)

salt and freshly ground black pepper

chopped fresh parsley, to garnish

1 Peel and finely chop the shallots or onion and the garlic. Chop the chilli (wear rubber gloves for protection). Cut the chicken into bite-sized pieces.

2 Heat the olive oil in a large saucepan. Add the chicken and cook over a high heat, turning constantly, until browned all over. Remove from the pan and set aside. Add the shallots or onion, garlic and chilli and cook for a few minutes until softened.

3 Return the chicken to the pan and add the thyme, tomatoes and wine. Bring to the boil, lower the heat and simmer for about 15 minutes or until the chicken is cooked right through.

4 Meanwhile, trim and roughly chop the courgettes, if using. Add the pasta to a large pan of boiling salted water and cook until *al dente*, or according to the packet instructions.

5 Add the courgettes and olives to the sauce, with the capers if using. Season with salt and pepper to taste. Simmer for 5 minutes or until the courgettes are just softened but still retain some bite.

6 Drain the pasta thoroughly in a colander. Serve immediately topped with the sauce and garnished with plenty of chopped parsley.

VARIATION
Halve 2 peppers and grill, cut-side down, until the skins are charred. Cover with a cloth and leave to cool slightly, then peel away the skins. Discard the cores and seeds, and cut the flesh into strips. Add to the sauce with the courgettes.

HERBED MUSHROOM RAVIOLI

Serves 6
Preparation: 55 minutes, plus resting
Cooking time: 5 minutes
Freezing: suitable
550 cals per serving

PASTA
200g (7oz) 'type 00' pasta flour, or strong white bread flour

pinch of salt

2 medium eggs

15ml (1 tbsp) olive oil

45ml (3 tbsp) mixed chopped fresh tarragon, marjoram and parsley

FILLING
2 shallots

225g (8oz) mixed wild mushrooms or 175g (6oz) dark flat mushrooms, plus 40g (1½oz) dried porcini

25g (1oz) black olives

4 sun-dried tomatoes in oil

50g (2oz) butter

15ml (1 tbsp) dry sherry

salt and freshly ground black pepper

freshly grated nutmeg

beaten egg, for brushing

TO SERVE
50g (2oz) butter, melted

few sautéed wild mushrooms

50g (2oz) Parmesan cheese

1 To make the pasta, sift the flour and salt into a mound on a clean work surface and make a well in the centre. Beat the eggs and oil together, then pour into the well. Sprinkle in the herbs. Gradually mix the liquid into the flour using one hand, then bring the dough together.

2 On a clean surface, with clean hands, knead the pasta for 5–10 minutes until smooth and elastic. Wrap in cling film and allow to rest at room temperature for 30 minutes.

3 For the filling, peel and finely chop the shallots. Wipe or brush the fresh mushrooms clean, then chop finely. If using dried mushrooms, soak in hot water to cover for 10–15 minutes. Remove and chop finely. Strain the soaking liquid through a filter paper and reserve. Stone and finely chop the olives. Drain and finely chop the sun-dried tomatoes.

4 Melt the butter in a pan, add the shallots and cook for 5 minutes until soft and golden. Add all the mushrooms, olives and dried tomatoes; cook, stirring, over a high heat for 1–2 minutes. Add the sherry and reserved liquid; cook for 1 minute. Season well with salt, pepper and nutmeg. Transfer to a bowl and leave to cool.

5 Now roll out the pasta dough (see pages 14–16). If using a pasta machine, roll manageable portions of dough into strips. If rolling out by hand, divide in half and roll into 2 sheets on a very lightly floured surface. Either way, roll out as thinly as possible and keep covered with a slightly damp tea towel.

6 Place 18 heaped spoonfuls of filling on one half of the pasta, spacing them at 4cm (1½ inch) intervals. Brush the dough in between with beaten egg. Lift the other sheet(s) of pasta over the top. Press down firmly between the pockets of filling and cut into 7.5cm (3 inch) squares. Transfer to a floured tea towel and leave to rest for 1 hour.

7 Bring a large pan of salted water to the boil, with a dash of oil added. Carefully add the ravioli, bring back to the boil, turn off the heat and cover with a tight-fitting lid. Leave for 5 minutes, then drain well. Serve immediately on warmed plates, topped with the melted butter, sautéed mushrooms and shavings of Parmesan.

SMOKED SALMON WITH DILL TAGLIATELLE

Serves 4

Preparation: 20–25 minutes, plus resting

Cooking time: 10 minutes for sauce; 2 minutes for pasta

Freezing: suitable – uncooked pasta only, in small quantities

970 cals per serving

1 quantity fresh herb pasta dough (see page 13) made with 50g (2oz) fresh dill sprigs

SAUCE
1 shallot

45ml (3 tbsp) white wine vinegar

225g (8oz) unsalted butter, chilled and cubed

salt and white pepper

squeeze of lemon juice

TO ASSEMBLE
225g (8oz) smoked salmon

40g (1½oz) butter, melted

dill sprigs and lemon wedges, to garnish

1 First make the pasta. Wrap the dough in cling film and allow to rest at room temperature for at least 30 minutes before rolling out.

2 Meanwhile, cut the smoked salmon into strips and set aside.

3 Using a pasta machine or a rolling pin, roll out the pasta dough very thinly in batches. Lay on floured tea towels and leave for 10 minutes to dry slightly. Cut the pasta into ribbons, either by machine or by hand (see pages 14–17). Leave the pasta to dry for 15 minutes on floured tea towels before cooking.

4 To make the butter sauce, finely chop the shallot and place in a small pan with 45ml (3 tbsp) water and the vinegar. Boil until reduced to 30ml (2 tbsp). Over a low heat, whisk in the butter, a piece at a time, until creamy and amalgamated (this process shouldn't take too long). Do not allow to boil or the sauce will separate. Season with salt and pepper, add the lemon juice and stir in the smoked salmon. Keep warm.

5 Bring a large pan of salted water to the boil and add the tagliatelle. Boil rapidly for 2 minutes or until *al dente*, then drain thoroughly. Toss the tagliatelle with the melted butter and divide between 4 warmed serving plates. Top with the smoked salmon in butter sauce. Garnish with sprigs of dill and lemon wedges. Serve at once.

VARIATION
If you prefer, flavour the sauce with other herbs such as chives or parsley instead of dill.

SPAGHETTI WITH MUSSELS

Serves 4
Preparation: 20 minutes
Cooking time: 35 minutes
Freezing: not suitable
575 cals per serving

900g (2lb) fresh mussels in shells

900g (2lb) really ripe fresh tomatoes

1 onion

4 garlic cloves, peeled

6 basil leaves

150ml (¼ pint) dry white wine

2 red chillies

30ml (2 tbsp) olive oil

salt and freshly ground black pepper

450g (1lb) dried spaghetti

small basil leaves, to garnish

1 Scrub the mussels thoroughly under cold running water and pull off the hairy 'beard' that protrudes from the shell. Discard any mussels with cracked or broken shells, and those that do not close when sharply tapped with the back of a knife.

2 Put the mussels into a large pan with a cupful of water. Cover with a tight-fitting lid and quickly bring to the boil. Cook for about 5 minutes, shaking the pan occasionally, until the mussels have opened. Transfer them to a bowl with a slotted spoon, discarding any unopened ones; set aside.

3 Strain the cooking juices through a muslin-lined sieve to remove any sand or grit; reserve.

4 Quarter the tomatoes and place them in a shallow saucepan. Peel and chop the onion; crush 2 of the garlic cloves. Add the onion and crushed garlic to the tomatoes with the basil. Bring to the boil and simmer for about 20 minutes until the tomatoes are beginning to disintegrate.

5 Press the tomato sauce through a nylon sieve or mouli to remove the seeds and skins. Return to the rinsed-out pan and pour in the reserved mussel liquid and wine. Bring to the boil and boil rapidly for 5 minutes or until reduced by about half.

6 Chop the other 2 garlic cloves; halve, deseed and chop the chillies. Heat the oil in another pan, add the garlic and chillies and cook until golden. Stir in the tomato sauce and mussels. Cover and simmer for 2–3 minutes until well heated through. Season with salt and pepper to taste.

7 Bring a large pan of salted water to the boil and add the spaghetti. Cook at a fast boil until *al dente*. Drain, holding back 30ml (2 tbsp) cooking liquid – this will help the sauce to cling to the pasta. Stir in the mussel sauce. Pile into a large warmed serving dish and sprinkle with basil leaves. Serve immediately.

TOP TIP
If you prefer not to have the shells in the dish, remove the cooked mussels from their shells at stage 2, when they are cool enough to handle.

PASTA WITH SCALLOPS AND GRILLED PEPPER PURÉE

Serves 4–6

Preparation: 20 minutes

Cooking time: 35 minutes

Freezing: suitable (red pepper purée only)

780–520 cals per serving

4 red peppers

6 unpeeled garlic cloves

450g (1lb) shelled medium scallops

75ml (5 tbsp) extra-virgin olive oil

5ml (1 tsp) paprika

coarse sea salt and freshly ground black pepper

400g (14oz) dried ribbon pasta, such as tagliatelle or papardelle

45ml (3 tbsp) chopped fresh parsley

15ml (1 tbsp) balsamic vinegar or lemon juice

60ml (4 tbsp) freshly grated Parmesan cheese

parsley sprigs, to garnish

1 Preheat the grill to hot. Place the whole peppers and unpeeled garlic cloves on the grill rack and grill, turning from time to time, until the peppers are blackened and blistered all over. This will take about 20 minutes, by which time the garlic cloves will be soft and tender in their papery skins. Allow to cool slightly.

2 Holding them over a bowl to catch the juices, peel the peppers, then remove the core and seeds. Peel the garlic. Chop the peppers roughly and put in a food processor with the garlic. Process for a few seconds to give a coarse purée; set aside.

3 Thread the scallops onto wooden skewers. Line the grill pan with foil to catch the juices. Brush the scallops with 30ml (2 tbsp) of the olive oil and sprinkle with the paprika. Season liberally with sea salt and pepper. Grill for 4–5 minutes, turning once halfway through cooking, until just firm. Remove the scallops from the skewers and slice any that are large.

4 Cook the pasta in a large pan of boiling salted water until *al dente*, or according to the packet instructions.

5 Meanwhile, transfer the pepper purée to a large frying pan. Heat gently, then stir in the scallops and the juices from the grill pan. Cook over a gentle heat for 1 minute, then stir in the parsley and balsamic vinegar or lemon juice. Remove from the heat.

6 Drain the pasta thoroughly in a colander and return to the pan. Add the remaining 45ml (3 tbsp) olive oil and toss to mix. Add the scallops in pepper sauce and toss again lightly. Serve at once, sprinkled with the Parmesan cheese and garnished with parsley.

TOP TIP

If you like spicy sauces, grill a red chilli along with the peppers to give the dish an extra 'kick'.

SHELLFISH PASTA WITH ROASTED CHERRY TOMATOES

Serves 4–6
Preparation: 30 minutes
Cooking time: 1–1¼ hours
Freezing: not suitable
760–505 cals per serving

4 medium-small onions

450g (1lb) cherry tomatoes

75ml (5 tbsp) extra-virgin olive oil

15ml (1 tbsp) chopped fresh thyme

salt and freshly ground black pepper

1kg (2lb) mussels in shells

12 large raw prawns

450g (1lb) squid

3–4 garlic cloves, peeled

175ml (6fl oz) dry white wine

chopped fresh parsley, to garnish

1 Preheat the oven to 200°C/400°F/gas 6. Peel the onions and cut each one into 6 wedges, leaving the root end intact. Arrange in one layer in a roasting tin. Halve the cherry tomatoes and arrange cut-side up in the tin. Drizzle over 45ml (3 tbsp) of the olive oil and sprinkle with thyme, salt and pepper. Roast in the oven for 1-1¼ hours until the onions are tender; the tomatoes will be soft.

2 Meanwhile, prepare the shellfish. Scrub and debeard the mussels, discarding any which do not close when firmly tapped with the back of a knife. Wash the prawns but leave them whole. Clean the squid pouch by washing it thoroughly under cold running water. Pull out the transparent 'quill' and then slice the squid.

3 About 20 minutes before serving, heat 30ml (2 tbsp) oil in a large saucepan. Roughly slice the garlic, add to the pan and cook over a medium heat for 1 minute. Add the wine and parsley stalks, bring to the boil and cook for 2 minutes.

4 Add the prawns to the pan and cook gently, covered, for 2 minutes. Add the squid and cook for a further 1–2 minutes until both are cooked. Transfer with a slotted spoon to a plate and set aside.

5 Add the mussels to the pan, cover and cook for 3–4 minutes, shaking the pan frequently, until they open. Strain, reserving the liquid but discarding the garlic and parsley. Discard any mussels which have not opened. Return all the cooked shellfish and the strained liquor to the pan.

6 Meanwhile, cook the pasta in a large pan of boiling salted water until almost *al dente*, about 1 minute less than the packet instructions. Drain thoroughly, and return to the pan. Add the shellfish and cooking liquor, toss to mix and heat through gently for 1 minute.

7 Add the roasted onion and cherry tomato mixture to the pan and toss lightly. Adjust the seasoning and serve at once, sprinkled with the chopped parsley.

PASTA WITH PRAWNS, MUSHROOMS AND WINE

Serves 4–6
Preparation: 30 minutes, plus 20 minutes
Cooking time: 12–15 minutes
Freezing: not suitable
675–450 cals per serving

15g (½oz) dried porcini mushrooms

16 large raw prawn tails in shells, about 450g (1lb) total weight

4 tomatoes

1 onion

25g (1oz) butter

60ml (4 tbsp) extra-virgin olive oil

2 garlic cloves, crushed

150ml (¼ pint) dry white wine

400g (14oz) large dried pasta shapes, such as shells, pipes or twists

salt and freshly ground black pepper

30ml (2 tbsp) chopped fresh parsley

tarragon leaves to garnish (optional)

1 Put the dried mushrooms in a small bowl and cover with 150ml (¼ pint) boiling water. Leave to soak for 20 minutes then drain, reserving the liquor, but take care to exclude any grit. Rinse the mushrooms and chop fairly finely.

2 'Butterfly' the prawns by snipping lengthways from head to tail, leaving the tail end intact. Set aside.

3 Immerse the tomatoes in boiling water for 30 seconds, cool slightly, then peel. Halve and deseed the tomatoes, then dice the flesh. Peel and chop the onion.

4 Heat the butter and oil in a large frying pan. Add the onion and cook for minutes, stirring frequently, until soft but not browned. Stir in the garlic and cook for a further minute, then add the prawns and mushrooms. Cook, stirring, for a few seconds, then pour in the wine and reserved mushroom liquor. Simmer for 2–3 minutes until the prawns are firm and cooked through.

5 Meanwhile, cook the pasta in a large pan of boiling salted water until *al dente*, according to the packet instructions.

6 Using a slotted spoon, transfer the prawns to a plate; set aside. Continue cooking the mushroom mixture until the liquid is reduced by half. Then stir in the tomatoes. Return the prawns to the pan and season with salt and pepper. Remove from the heat until the pasta is ready.

7 Drain the pasta thoroughly and transfer to a warmed large serving bowl. Gently reheat the sauce if necessary and stir in the parsley. Add to the pasta and toss lightly to mix. Serve at once, sprinkle with tarragon leaves if desired.

VARIATION
For a rich, creamy version, add 150ml (¼ pint) double cream to the pan after removing the prawns. Reduce the liquid by half in the same way. Finish as above.

CRAB-FILLED PASTA SHELLS

Serves 4
Preparation: 30 minutes
Cooking time: about 30 minutes
Freezing: not suitable
765 cals per serving

450g (1lb) prepared crabmeat
(shell and claws reserved)

300ml (½ pint) dry white wine

1 lemon grass stalk, grated

60ml (4 tbsp) crème fraîche
(optional)

20 large dried pasta shells
(conchiglioni)

25g (1oz) butter

1 shallot, peeled and finely
chopped

2 red chillies, seeded and finely
diced

15g (¼oz) basil leaves (from
1 plant), finely shredded

salt and freshly ground black
pepper

30–40ml (2–3 tbsp) fresh
breadcrumbs

45ml (3 tbsp) freshly grated
Parmesan cheese

olive oil, for drizzling

basil sprigs, to garnish

1 Put the crab claws and shells in a saucepan with the wine, 300ml (½ pint) water and the lemon grass. Bring to the boil, cover and simmer for 15 minutes to make a stock. Strain, then return to the pan. Boil to reduce by one-third. Stir in the crème fraîche, if using. Set aside.

2 Cook the pasta in a large pan of boiling salted water until *al dente*. Drain thoroughly in a colander. Arrange the pasta shells upside-down on a board to dry. Preheat the oven to 220°C/425°F/gas 7.

3 Melt the butter in a large frying pan. Add the shallot and chillies and sauté over a medium heat for 4–5 minutes to soften; do not brown. Stir in the shredded basil and cook until wilted, then remove from the heat. Add the flaked crabmeat. Mix gently and season with salt and pepper to taste.

4 Mix together the breadcrumbs and Parmesan. Fill the pasta shells with the crab mixture and place in a large baking dish. Pour the reserved stock or sauce around the shells. Sprinkle the breadcrumb mixture over the crab filling and drizzle with olive oil. Cover and cook in the oven for 15 minutes, removing the lid for the last 5 minutes.

5 Transfer the crab-filled shells to warmed serving plates and spoon the sauce or reduced stock around them. Garnish with basil and serve at once.

PASTA SHELLS WITH SALMON AND DILL

Serves 4–6
Preparation: 15 minutes
Cooking time: 18–20 minutes
Freezing: not suitable
1000–670 cals per serving

300g (10oz) fresh salmon fillet, skinned

125g (4oz) sliced smoked salmon

1 onion

40g (1½oz) butter

250ml (8fl oz) dry white wine

30ml (2 tbsp) wholegrain mustard

300ml (½ pint) extra-thick double cream

30–45ml (2–3 tbsp) chopped fresh dill

salt and freshly ground black pepper

400g (14oz) dried pasta shells

TO GARNISH
dill sprigs

toasted pine nuts, for sprinkling (optional)

1 Cut the fresh salmon fillet into 2.5cm (1 inch) cubes. Cut the smoked salmon into strips. Set both aside. Peel and chop the onion.

2 Melt the butter in a large frying pan. Add the onion and cook over a medium heat for about 7 minutes until soft and golden. Stir in the wine and mustard and bring to the boil. Cook for 5–7 minutes until reduced by half.

3 Stir in the cream and continue cooking for 1 minute, then lower the heat and add the fresh salmon to the pan. Cook gently for 2–3 minutes until the fish is firm. Stir in the dill and season with salt and pepper. Remove from the heat.

4 Meanwhile, cook the pasta in a large pan of boiling salted water until *al dente*, according to the packet instructions. Drain thoroughly, then transfer to a warmed serving dish.

5 To serve, gently reheat the sauce if necessary. Add to the pasta with the smoked salmon strips and toss lightly to mix. Serve at once, garnished with tiny sprigs of dill and sprinkled with toasted pine nuts, if wished.

VARIATION
Substitute creamed horseradish in place of the wholegrain mustard. As the intensity of flavour varies between brands, begin by adding 1 tablespoon, then taste and add more to your liking.

TOP TIP
Use kitchen scissors to snip the smoked salmon slices into strips.

SMOKED FISH RAVIOLINI IN A CREAM SAUCE

Serves 4–6
Preparation: 45 minutes
Cooking time: about 20 minutes
Freezing: suitable at end of stage 5
970–650 cals per serving

1 quantity basic pasta dough (see pages 12–13)

FILLING
575g (1¼ lb) smoked haddock fillet

15ml (1 tbsp) olive oil

1 small onion

15g (½ oz) butter

125g (4oz) ricotta cheese, if available, or cream cheese

2 egg yolks

30ml (2 tbsp) chopped fresh parsley

SAUCE
15g (½ oz) butter

125g (4oz) frozen peas

300ml (½ pint) extra-thick double cream

75ml (5 tbsp) freshly grated Parmesan cheese

salt and freshly ground black pepper

TO GARNISH
30ml (2 tbsp) snipped chives

1 First make the pasta dough. Wrap in cling film to prevent the dough drying out and leave to rest for 15–20 minutes.

2 To make the filling, brush the fish all over with the olive oil and grill, skin-side up to prevent the flesh from drying out, without turning, for 5–10 minutes until the flesh is firm and opaque. The exact cooking time will depend on the thickness of the fillet. Remove the skin and any bones. Flake the flesh using a fork and place in a bowl.

3 Meanwhile, peel and finely chop the onion. Melt the butter in a small frying pan. Add the onion and cook over a medium heat for about 5 minutes until soft but not browned.

4 Add the onion to the fish with the ricotta or cream cheese, egg yolks and parsley. Mix well with the fork and season with salt and pepper; salt should not be necessary. Set aside.

5 Roll out half of the pasta dough as thinly as possible (see pages 14–16). Using a metal 7.5cm (3 inch) round fluted cutter, stamp out circles of dough. Divide half of the filling between the pasta circles. Moisten the edges with a little water and fold each in half to form filled semi-circular parcels. Press the edges lightly to seal. Repeat with the remaining pasta dough and filling. You should be able to make about 60 raviolini.

6 To make the sauce, melt the butter in a frying pan, add the peas and cook on a medium heat for 3 minutes. Stir in the cream and bring to the boil. Remove from the heat. Meanwhile, cook the pasta in a large pan of boiling salted water for 2–3 minutes until *al dente*. Drain thoroughly and transfer to warmed serving plates.

7 To serve, gently reheat the sauce and stir in the Parmesan cheese. Season to taste. Pour over the raviolini and toss gently. Serve at once, sprinkled with chives.

LINGUINI WITH MONKFISH AND GRILLED CHILLIS

Serves 4–6
Preparation: 20 minutes
Cooking time: about 20 minutes
Freezing: not suitable
605–405 cals per serving

450g (1lb) monkfish, filleted

6–8 large red chillis

1 onion

3 garlic cloves

15g (½ oz) butter

60ml (4 tbsp) extra-virgin olive oil

30ml (2 tbsp) capers, rinsed and drained

finely grated rind of 1 small lemon

400g (14oz) dried linguini or capellini

45ml (3 tbsp) chopped fresh coriander

10ml (2 tsp) chopped fresh mint

15ml (1 tbsp) balsamic vinegar or lemon juice

salt and freshly ground black pepper

coriander leaves, to garnish

1 Cut the monkfish fillet into thin slices and set aside.

2 Preheat the grill to hot. Grill the whole chillis, turning occasionally, until their skins are blackened and blistered all over; this will take about 10 minutes. Carefully remove and discard the skins, slit each chilli open lengthways and rinse out the seeds under cold running water. Dry on kitchen paper. Cut the flesh lengthways into thin strips.

3 Peel and chop the onion; peel and thinly slice the garlic. Heat the butter and oil in a large frying pan. Add the onion and cook over a medium heat for 5 minutes, stirring frequently, until softened but not brown. Stir in the garlic and cook for a further minute.

4 Increase the heat to medium-high and add the monkfish to the pan. Cook, stirring, for 3–4 minutes until the fish is firm and opaque. Lower the heat and stir in the capers, chilli strips and lemon rind. Remove from the heat until the pasta is ready.

5 Meanwhile, cook the pasta in a large pan of boiling salted water until *al dente*, according to the packet instructions. Drain thoroughly in a colander.

6 Heat the monkfish through gently, then remove from the heat and stir in the coriander, mint and balsamic vinegar or lemon juice. Season with salt and pepper to taste. Add the pasta and toss lightly to mix. Serve at once

TOP TIP
Large chillis are milder than small ones and much of their fiery heat is tempered when they are grilled and skinned.

VARIATION
Substitute 350g (12oz) peeled prawns for the monkfish reducing the cooking as follows: do not increase the heat when adding the prawns and heat for only 1 minute before adding the chillis and lemon rind. Then continue as above.

PASTA WITH CHICKEN LIVERS AND PEAS

Serves 4–6
Preparation: 15 minutes
Cooking time: about 20 minutes
Freezing: not suitable
690–460 cals per serving

450g (1lb) chicken livers

3 shallots or 1 small onion

1 garlic clove

50g (2oz) smoked pancetta, in one piece, or smoked streaky bacon

40g (1½oz) butter

30ml (2 tbsp) finely chopped fresh parsley

120ml (4fl oz) dry white wine

50g (2oz) frozen petits pois or peas, thawed

90ml (6 tbsp) fromage frais (40% fat)

salt and freshly ground black pepper

400g (14oz) tagliatelle, preferably fresh plain or garlic and herb pasta

TO FINISH
20ml (4 tsp) fromage frais

1 Rinse and drain the chicken livers. Chop them roughly, discarding any fibrous bits. Peel and chop the shallots or onion and crush the garlic.

2 Cut the rind from the pancetta or bacon and slice into small strips or 'lardons'. Cook in a small pan, without any extra fat, over a medium heat for 4–5 minutes until the pancetta or bacon is lightly browned and just crisp. Transfer to a plate and set aside.

3 Melt 25g (1oz) of the butter in a large frying pan. Add the shallots or onion and garlic and cook over a medium heat, stirring frequently, for about 5 minutes until softened but not brown.

4 Increase the heat and add the chicken livers to the pan. Cook, stirring frequently, for 4–5 minutes until browned and sealed. Stir in the parsley and wine and continue cooking over a high heat for 3 minutes or until about two-thirds of the liquid has evaporated, leaving a rich sauce. Stir in the peas.

5 Meanwhile, cook the tagliatelle until *al dente*. For dried pasta, cook according to the packet instructions. If using fresh pasta, cook for 2–3 minutes only.

6 Drain the pasta thoroughly and return to the pan with the remaining 15g (½oz) butter. Toss to mix.

7 Add the fromage frais to the chicken livers and cook, stirring, for 2–3 minutes on a medium heat. Remove from the heat and season with salt and pepper.

8 Serve the pasta on individual plates topped with the chicken liver mixture. Add a spoonful of fromage frais to each serving and sprinkle with the reserved pancetta or bacon.

TOP TIP
Trim away any membranes and tubes from the chicken livers before cutting them into smaller pieces.

PAPPARDELLE WITH FRAZZLED PROSCIUTTO AND ASPARAGUS

Serves 4–6
Preparation: 30 minutes
Cooking time: about 12 minutes
Freezing: not suitable
850–565 cals per serving

350g (12oz) frozen young broad beans, thawed

3 shallots

2 garlic cloves

350g (12oz) asparagus

90ml (6 tbsp) extra-virgin olive oil

175g (6oz) prosciutto or Parma ham, in thin slices

400g (14oz) dried papardelle or other pasta ribbons

45ml (3 tbsp) chopped fresh parsley

salt and freshly ground black pepper

300g (10oz) goat's cheese log, with rind

1 Slip the broad beans out of their waxy outer skins into a bowl and set aside. Peel and finely chop the shallots; crush the garlic.

2 Trim the asparagus, discarding any woody parts of the stems. Cook in shallow boiling water for about 4 minutes until almost tender. Drain and refresh under cold running water. Cut into 5cm (2 inch) lengths and set aside.

3 Heat the oil in a large frying pan. Add the prosciutto, in batches if necessary, and fry over a high heat for a few seconds. Lift out onto a plate and set aside. Add the shallots and garlic to the frying pan and cook gently for 5 minutes to soften; do not allow to brown. Increase the heat to medium and add the broad beans. Cook, stirring, for 4 minutes.

4 Cook the pasta in a large pan of boiling salted water until *al dente*, according to the packet instructions.

5 While the pasta is cooking, preheat the grill to hot. Add the asparagus to the frying pan with the parsley. Cook, stirring, for 2 minutes, then return the prosciutto to the pan. Season with salt and pepper. Remove from the heat.

6 Meanwhile, cut the goat's cheese into slices and arrange on a lightly greased baking sheet. Grill for 3–4 minutes until lightly browned.

7 Drain the pasta thoroughly. Gently reheat the prosciutto mixture if necessary, then lightly toss with the pasta in the large pan. Arrange on serving plates and top with the grilled goat's cheese. Serve at once.

TOP TIP
If you want a less substantial dish, cook it without the goat's cheese. The results still taste delicious.

VARIATION
Replace the broad beans with 75g (3oz) fresh rocket. Add to the pan with the asparagus and parsley.

TAGLIATELLE WITH BROAD BEANS, CHICORY AND CREAM

Serves 4–6
Preparation: 25 minutes
Cooking time: 10 minutes
Freezing: not suitable
880–590 cals per serving

350g (12oz) frozen broad beans, thawed

1 onion

40g (1½oz) butter

2 heads chicory, total weight about 200g (7oz)

400g (14oz) dried white and green tagliatelle or freshly made tagliatelle

45ml (3 tbsp) chopped fresh parsley or chervil

300ml (½ pint) extra-thick double cream

60ml (4 tbsp) freshly grated Parmesan cheese

salt and freshly ground black pepper

TO SERVE
extra herbs and Parmesan cheese

1 Remove the waxy outer skins from the broad beans by pinching one end and discard. Put the bright green beans into a bowl and set aside. Peel and finely chop the onion.

2 Melt the butter in a large frying pan. Add the onion and cook over a medium heat, stirring frequently, for 5–6 minutes until soft. Slice the chicory.

3 Cook the pasta in a large pan of boiling salted water until *al dente*, according to the packet instructions.

4 Meanwhile, add the broad beans to the onion in the frying pan and continue cooking for 2 minutes, then stir in the chicory slices and parsley or chervil. Cook for a further 2 minutes, then stir in the cream. Bring to the boil and add the grated Parmesan. Season with salt and pepper to taste.

5 Drain the pasta thoroughly and transfer to a warmed serving dish. Add the sauce and toss to mix. Serve at once, sprinkled with extra herbs and shavings of Parmesan cheese.

VARIATION
Replace the broad beans with 300g (10oz) frozen peas. Add them to the onion with the chicory.

PASTA WITH SMOKED TROUT, PEPPERS AND ALMONDS

Serves 4–6
Preparation: 20 minutes
Cooking time: about 30 minutes
Freezing: not suitable
785–525 cals per serving

3 large red peppers

225g (8oz) smoked trout fillets

60ml (4 tbsp) extra-virgin olive oil

75g (3oz) flaked almonds

400g (14oz) dried pasta bows, shells or pipes

45ml (3 tbsp) chopped fresh dill

40g (1½oz) butter

salt and freshly ground black pepper

dill sprigs, to garnish

1 Preheat the grill to hot. Grill the peppers whole, turning occasionally, until the skins are charred and blistered all over. This will take about 20 minutes. Allow to cool slightly, then over a bowl to catch any juices, remove the skins. Cut the peppers into thin strips, discarding the seeds.

2 Flake the smoked trout fillets. Heat the oil in a large frying pan. Add the flaked almonds and cook over a medium heat for about 3 minutes until lightly browned.

3 Meanwhile, cook the pasta in a large pan of boiling salted water until *al dente*, according to the packet instructions.

4 Add the pepper strips and any reserved juices to the almonds. Heat through for 1 minute, then stir in the chopped dill and flaked trout. Heat for 1 minute, then remove from the heat and stir in the butter – this will prevent any further cooking. Season with salt and pepper to taste.

5 To serve, drain the pasta thoroughly. Add to the smoked trout mixture and toss lightly to mix. Serve immediately, garnished with dill.

TOP TIP

To save time, cut the peppers into quarters before grilling. Grill the pieces skin-side up for about 10 minutes until they are blistered and blackened. The drawback with this method is that the sweet juices are not retained within the cooked peppers.

FETTUCINE WITH GORGONZOLA AND SPINACH

Preparation: about 15 minutes
Cooking time: 10 minutes
Freezing: not suitable
630–420 cals per serving

350g (12oz) young leaf spinach

225g (8oz) gorgonzola cheese

75ml (3 fl oz) milk

25g (1oz) butter

salt and freshly ground black pepper

400g (14oz) fettucine, tagliatelle or long fusilli

freshly grated nutmeg, to serve

1 Wash the spinach thoroughly and remove any large stalks. Place in a clean saucepan and cook, stirring, over a medium-high heat for 2–3 minutes until wilted. There is no need to add extra water – the small amount clinging to the leaves after washing provides sufficient moisture. Drain well in a colander or sieve, pressing out any excess liquid.

2 Cut the gorgonzola into small pieces. Place in a clean pan with the milk and butter. Heat gently, stirring, until melted to a creamy sauce. Stir in the drained spinach. Season to taste with pepper; salt may not be necessary because the gorgonzola is quite salty.

3 Just before serving, cook the pasta in a large pan of boiling salted water until *al dente*, according to the packet instructions. (Fresh pasta will require only 2–3 minutes' cooking time.)

4 Drain the pasta thoroughly and add to the sauce. Toss well to mix. Serve at once, sprinkled with a little freshly grated nutmeg.

VARIATIONS
● *Add 125g (4oz) cooked smoked ham, cut into small dice or fine strips, to the sauce with the wilted spinach.*
● *As an alternative to gorgonzola, make the dish with dolcelatte cheese, which will provide a milder, sweeter flavour.*

TOP TIP
To drain the spinach thoroughly, press it in a colander or sieve with the back of a wooden spoon.

PASTA WITH CHILLI BEEF

Serves 4
Preparation: 10–15 minutes
Cooking time: about 10 minutes
Freezing: not suitable
409 cals per serving

30ml (2 tbsp) olive oil

450g (1lb) rump steak, trimmed and cut into bite-sized pieces

225g (8oz) red pepper, seeded and cut into bite-sized pieces

225g (8oz) broccoli, stalks sliced and head cut into florets

115g (4oz) onion, peeled and chopped

2.5 ml (½ tsp) chilli powder, or a few drops of Tabasco sauce

10ml (2 tsp) dried oregano or other dried mixed herbs

50g (2oz) dried tagliarini, spaghettini or other thin noodles

30ml (2 tbsp) sherry or medium white wine

300ml (10fl oz) beef stock

15ml (1 tbsp) soy sauce

freshly ground black pepper

fresh oregano, to garnish

1 Heat the oil in a large saucepan and brown the beef well on all sides for about 2–3 minutes. Remove with a slotted spoon.

2 Add all the vegetables, chilli powder and oregano and cook, stirring, for 1–2 minutes.

3 Mix in the pasta, sherry, stock and soy sauce. Cover and simmer for about 5 minutes, or until the pasta and broccoli are tender.

4 Return the beef to the pan. Bring to the boil, then simmer for 1 minute to heat through. Season with pepper and serve immediately, garnished with fresh oregano.

BLACK PEPPERCORN PAPARDELLE WITH SALMON AND SAFFRON CREAM

Serves 4
Preparation: 20 minutes, plus pasta
Cooking time: 15–20 minutes
Freezing: suitable
840 cals per serving

150ml (¼ pint) hot vegetable stock

2.5ml (½ tsp) saffron threads

225g (8oz) shelled broad beans

125g (4oz) shelled peas

50g (2oz) unsalted butter

2 shallots, peeled and finely chopped

1 small garlic clove, peeled and crushed

90ml (3fl oz) dry white wine

150ml (¼ pint) double cream

30ml (2 tbsp) chopped fresh dill

350g (12oz) skinless salmon fillet

1 quantity fresh black peppercorn pappardelle (see pages13–18), or 400g (14oz) dried pappardelle

salt and freshly ground black pepper

1 Pour the hot stock into a bowl, add the saffron threads and leave to infuse for 10 minutes. Blanch the broad beans in lightly salted boiling water for 1 minute; drain, refresh under cold water and pat dry. Squeeze the beans out of their tough outer skins. Blanch the peas for 1 minute; drain, refresh under cold water and dry well.

2 Melt half of the butter in a saucepan, add the shallots and garlic and sauté over a low heat for 5 minutes until softened but not coloured.

3 Add the wine and boil rapidly until reduced to about 15ml (1 tbsp), then add the infused stock and boil for 3 minutes. Stir in the cream and simmer for a further 4–5 minutes until thickened. Remove from the heat and stir in the dill.

4 Meanwhile, melt the remaining butter in a large heavy-based frying pan. Add the salmon fillet and fry for 3 minutes on each side until golden. Remove from the pan and leave until cool enough to handle, then roughly flake the fish.

5 Pour the saffron cream into the frying pan (used to cook the salmon). Stir in the beans and peas and heat through for 5 minutes.

6 While this is heating, cook the pasta in a large pan of boiling salted water for 1–2 minutes until *al dente*.

7 Drain the pasta, add to the sauce and toss well. Season with salt and pepper to taste and immediately spoon the papardelle into individual bowls. Top each serving with the flaked fish and serve at once.

SAFFRON TAGLIATELLE WITH RED MULLET AND HOT PEPPER SAUCE

Serves 4
Preparation: 20 minutes, plus pasta
Cooking time: 15 minutes
Freezing: not suitable
1110 cals per serving

25g (1oz) butter

1 onion, peeled and thinly sliced

300ml (½ pint) double cream

5 garlic cloves, peeled and crushed

4 strips of pared orange rind

several sprigs of fresh thyme

2 bay leaves

1 quantity fresh saffron tagliatelle (see pages 14–17), or 400g (14oz) dried

salt and freshly ground black pepper

8 red mullet fillets

PEPPER PASTE
1 large red pepper, cored, seeded and roughly chopped

1 red chilli, seeded and roughly chopped

15g (½oz) fresh white breadcrumbs

75ml (5 tbsp) olive oil

TO GARNISH
thyme sprigs

1 First make the pepper paste. Put the red pepper and chilli in a food processor and work to a paste. Add the breadcrumbs, 15ml (1 tbsp) of the oil and a little salt and blend until smooth. Gradually blend in the remaining oil to make a paste. Turn into a serving dish.

2 Melt the butter in a frying pan, add the onion and fry gently for about 5 minutes.

3 At the same time, put the cream, garlic, orange rind, thyme and bay leaves in a small saucepan. Heat gently for 5 minutes.

4 Meanwhile, cook the pasta in a large pan of boiling salted water until *al dente*; fresh pasta will only take 1–2 minutes.

5 Pat the red mullet fillets dry with kitchen paper. Add to the frying pan and fry for 1 minute on each side until cooked through.

6 Drain the pasta and return to the pan. Add the onions, red mullet, cream sauce and seasoning and heat through gently. Serve scattered with thyme sprigs and spoonfuls of the pepper sauce.

TOP TIP
Any firm-textured fish can be used in this recipe. Try filleted pieces of skinned monkfish, halibut or sea bass.

DEEP-FRIED RIGATONI WITH SOY DIPPING SAUCE

Serves 4

Preparation: 40-45 minutes

Cooking time: about 20 minutes

Freezing: rigatoni suitable (at end of stage 5; deep-fry from frozen)

1015 cals per serving

20–30 dried rigatoni tubes (depending on size)

salt and freshly ground black pepper

FILLING

250g (8oz) ricotta cheese

6 large spring onions, white part only, finely chopped

2.5cm (1 inch) fresh root ginger, peeled and finely diced

125g (4oz) creamed coconut, grated

finely grated rind of 1 lime

½ plump red chilli, seeded and finely chopped

30ml (2 tbsp) chopped fresh coriander leaves

1 egg yolk

DIPPING SAUCE

15ml (1 tbsp) sesame oil

30ml (2 tbsp) soy sauce

30ml (2 tbsp) red wine vinegar

juice of 1 lime

30ml (2 tbsp) stem ginger syrup, or sugar to taste

½ plump red chilli, finely diced

TO FINISH

plain white flour, for coating

1 egg white, beaten with 15ml (1 tbsp) water

150–175g (5–6oz) day-old white breadcrumbs

1 Mix all the ingredients for the filling together in a bowl and season with salt and pepper to taste. Cover and refrigerate until required.

2 Cook the rigatoni tubes in a large pan of boiling salted water for about 10 minutes or until just *al dente*. (If overcooked they may tear when they are filled.) Drain and refresh in cold water. Drain again and spread out on a clean tea towel to dry.

3 To make the dipping sauce, mix all the ingredients together in a bowl and set aside to allow the flavours to blend.

4 Use a piping bag fitted with a large plain nozzle to fill the rigatoni. Spoon half of the filling into the bag. Pipe the mixture into the pasta tubes, blocking the bottom end with one finger as you do so; do not overfill. Repeat to fill the remaining rigatoni.

5 Toss the stuffed rigatoni in the flour, shaking off any excess. Dip into the egg white, then in the breadcrumbs to coat evenly, shaking off any excess. Place the rigatoni on a tray and refrigerate for about 20 minutes.

6 Divide the dipping sauce between 4 tiny serving bowls and set aside.

7 Heat a 7.5cm (3 inch) depth of oil or fat in a deep-fat fryer or deep saucepan to 160°C (325°F), or until a cube of stale bread sizzles as soon as it is dropped in. Deep-fry the rigatoni in batches, 5–6 at a time, for about 2 minutes until golden brown and crisp. Remove and drain on kitchen paper; keep warm in a low oven while cooking the remainder.

8 Arrange the deep-fried rigatoni on warmed serving plates with frisée or shredded lettuce. Garnish with coriander sprigs and lime wedges and serve at once with the dipping sauce.

> TOP TIP
>
> These make an unusual starter. Prepare and deep-fry the rigatoni in advance, then reheat in the oven at 200°C/400°F/gas 6 for 15 minutes.

BUCKWHEAT PASTA WITH GRILLED RADICCHIO

Serves 4
Preparation: 20 minutes, plus pasta
Cooking time: 15 minutes
Freezing: not suitable
575 cals per serving

60ml (4 tbsp) extra-virgin olive oil, plus extra for brushing

2 small red onions, peeled and thinly sliced

1 garlic clove, peeled and crushed

15ml (1 tbsp) chopped fresh thyme

pinch of sugar

2 heads of radicchio, cut into thick wedges

1 quantity fresh buckwheat tagliatelle (see pages 13–17), or 400g (14oz) dried

salt and freshly ground black pepper

30ml (2 tbsp) balsamic vinegar

25g (1oz) capers in wine vinegar, drained

50g (2oz) pine nuts, toasted

basil leaves, to garnish

freshly grated Parmesan cheese, to taste (optional)

1 Heat the 60ml (4 tbsp) oil in a deep frying pan, add the garlic, thyme and sugar and fry for 10–15 minutes until golden and tender.

2 Meanwhile, preheat the grill. (If using dry pasta, which takes 10–12 minutes to cook, start cooking it in a large pan of boiling salted water now.) Lay the radicchio wedges on the grill rack, brush with a little oil and grill for 2–3 minutes. Turn the wedges over, brush with oil and grill for a further 2–3 minutes until charred and tender; keep warm.

3 Cook the buckwheat pasta in a large pan of boiling salted water until *al dente*; fresh pasta will take only 2–3 minutes.

4 Add the balsamic vinegar, capers, nuts and basil to the onions and stir well; keep warm.

5 Drain the pasta, reserving 60ml (4 tbsp) water. Add both to the onions with the radicchio. Stir briefly over a medium heat, then season with salt and pepper. Serve at once, garnished with basil and accompanied by Parmesan cheese, if liked.

INDEX